the Miracle Match

the Miracle Match

WACA Ground, 12 December 1976

IAN BRAYSHAW

hardie grant books

MELBOURNE · LONDON

To all who contributed—before, during and after—to what was a truly amazing, unforgettable day.

Published in 2014 by Hardie Grant Books

Hardie Grant Books (Australia)
Ground Floor, Building 1
658 Church Street
Richmond, Victoria 3121
www.hardiegrant.com.au

Hardie Grant Books (UK)
5th & 6th Floor
52–54 Southwark Street
London SE1 1RU
www.hardiegrant.co.uk

Cataloguing in publications data is available from the National
Library of Australia
The Miracle Match
ISBN 978 1 74270 933 8

Cover design by Luke Causby
Text design by Patrick Cannon
Cover photograph Newspix
Typeset in Palatino 11.25/17 pt by Cannon Typesetting
Printed and bound in Australia by Griffin Press

The paper this book is printed on is certified against the Forest
Stewardship Council® Standards. Griffin Press holds FSC
chain of custody certification SGS-COC-005088. FSC promotes
environmentally responsible, socially beneficial and economically
viable management of the world's forests.

FSC
www.fsc.org
MIX
Paper from
responsible sources
FSC® C009448

Contents

Author's note   *ix*

Prologue   *xi*

A classic showdown   1

The short form   3

Setting the scene   7

Lightning fast   10

Frozen butter   13

Heads or tails?   16

Stumpy and Grumpy   19

Slingshot superstar   25

Let play begin   43

A flawed diamond   53

The floodgates open   65

Quick-change act   70

A false dawn 75

No appetite 81

Demon Dennis 86

Master Blaster 102

Head-on collision 122

Mr Elegance 138

The gloveman 158

A clever plan 176

A change of mood 183

The Godfather 190

Battle lines 194

The wild one 197

Two wickets left 200

Can you believe it? 208

Aftermath 215

Finis piece 221

Acknowledgements 225

About the author 227

Author's note

Many interviews have been executed in the preparation of this book. In the interests of recognition, when an individual is quoted, here is the list of the personnel involved with the game:

Queensland players—Greg ('Tears') Chappell (captain),
John ('OGO') Maclean (vice-captain), Viv ('Smoky') Richards,
Alan ('Jonesey') Jones, David ('Rags') Ogilvie, Phil ('Port')
Carlson, Jeff ('Jilbert') Langley, Graham ('Grimace') Whyte,
Jeff ('Two-Up') Thomson, Denis ('Louie') Schuller, Geoff
('Mary') Dymock and Malcolm ('Mal') Francke (12th man)

Western Australia players—Rod ('Bacchus') Marsh (captain),
Dennis ('FOT') Lillee (vice-captain), Bruce ('Stumpy')
Laird, Ric ('Grumpy') Charlesworth, Rob ('Tables') Langer,

Kim ('Clag') Hughes, Craig ('Sarge') Serjeant, Ian ('Sticks') Brayshaw, Bruce ('Roo') Yardley, Mick ('Sos') Malone, Wayne ('Dunny') Clark and Bob ('Cocky') Paulsen (12th man)

Umpires—Gary Duperouzel and Don Hawks

Western Australia team squad co-ordinator—Daryl Foster

Western Australia selectors—Allan Edwards and Lawrie Sawle

Channel 9 commentators—Richie Benaud, Bob Simpson, Bill Lawry and Ian Chappell

Prologue

'When you pulled your spike through to make your mark it was almost slippery.'—Western Australia opening batsman Ric Charlesworth, on marking his guard on the controversial WACA Ground greentop.

'I sensed that for us to win, Viv and I would have to get the bulk of the runs.'—Greg Chappell before the run chase, knowing that Dennis Lillee would be fired up on a lightning-fast wicket.

'There's a big crowd here. Let's not let them down. Let's make 'em fight for it.'—Rod Marsh to his team, before going out to defend the Western Australian total.

'Make 'em fight for it, be buggered. We're going to beat these bastards!'—Dennis Lillee, before going out to spearhead the Western Australia bowling attack.

'Poor old John Maclean. He survived Dennis Lillee, but he couldn't survive Denis Schuller!'—Bill Lawry, television commentator, after Denis Schuller had run out his vice-captain.

'If WA can win this, it will be one of the great results in Australian cricket.'—Richie Benaud, television commentator.

'Do I remember that game? It's never far from the mind, man!'—West Indies great Sir Vivian Richards, who opened the batting for Queensland.

A classic showdown

When it comes to swagger and oozing outward self-confidence, there have been few in world cricket to equal Viv Richards. His act simply begged the bowler to 'bring it on, man'. And so often did the best in the business try to do just that, only to find who the master really was.

One of those rare moments when Viv Richards was fully put to the test was during an extraordinary limited-overs match that took place at the Western Australian Cricket Association (WACA) Ground in Perth in 1976. Twelve months earlier, a twenty-three-year-old Richards had set the same ground alight with a blazing 175 for the West Indies against Western Australia (WA)—an innings that included some amazing power hitting. Now he was back, this time playing for Queensland in a brief invitation stint, and well on the way to being recognised as one of the finest batsmen of all time.

It was the Gillette Cup domestic one-day cricket tournament semifinal, and when Richards walked out to face the first ball, he was confident he could dominate his opponents the same way he had a year before, and run down a paltry run chase on his own. The home side desperately needed to find a way to take the swagger out of the 'Master Blaster' if they were to have a chance.

At that time there was arguably only one man, not just in WA, or even Australia, but the entire cricketing world, who possessed the ability and the inspiration to take on the challenge. And as Viv casually reached the middle to take the first ball, *he* was measuring out his run at the River End: Dennis Lillee.

Preparing to tackle a cricketing version of 'Mission: Impossible', Lillee charged in to impose his will on a grim situation for his team, and take on Richards head to head. What would follow is one of the most amazing beginnings to an innings in any form of cricket—in a game that would come to be remembered as 'The Miracle Match'.

The short form

If there are intrinsic—dare we say it, old-fashioned—values in four- and five-day cricket, then the short form in its 40 years of existence has provided a distinctly different beat. Like switching from a Mozart concerto to Queen hammering out 'We will rock you!'—a nice cosy room, comfy slippers and a cardigan versus a thumping music arena with speakers blaring and the blood pulsating. The limited-overs game was introduced in English County cricket in 1963 as a potential saviour for flagging clubs' finances, and the Gillette Cup tournament was established. The Cup was soon introduced in Australia too, and it was a runaway success. At least in the medium term. In both countries there have been several name changes since, but the immediacy of the one-day format introduced new life and vigour to the game, attracting a new audience—women and children. And sending the turnstiles whirling.

In the prime of limited-overs cricket in England, there were as many as three competitions. While the popularity of the game increased, however, concerns were expressed that this 'hit-and-giggle' game would be the end of cricket's dyed-in-the-wool adherence to technique. And there was merit in the concern. The pressure to score quickly encouraged batsmen to contradict the norms in pursuit of penetrating a gap in the field—of making runs in a hurry. In those days there was nothing to prevent a captain placing all of his fieldsmen on the boundary in an attempt to stem the flow of runs. In one particular game, an English captain even had his 'keeper on the boundary. The great Barry Richards once told me that, playing one-dayers for Hampshire in the County competition, to score a boundary he'd been forced to develop a new shot to the defensive pace bowler: glide the ball just wide of the wicketkeeper and just fine of the third man. Victory was so important!

The first One Day International game (ODI) was played at the Melbourne Cricket Ground (MCG) on 5 January 1971—an idea put into play after the Third Test at that ground between Australia and England had been abandoned without a ball being bowled. However, the short form really hit the international stage in 1972, with the scheduling of three games between England and Australia as part of the Ashes tour of England. Three years later, the first of the World Cup tournaments (of 60 overs) was staged in England—when the West Indies scored a narrow victory over Australia in a final played before a lockout crowd at Lord's.

How well I remember the beginnings of the domestic limited-overs competition in Australia. It was the 1969–70 season, with 40 eight-ball overs. New Zealand fielded a team, entering at the semifinals stage, and defeated Victoria in the final. We players had heard about this hit-and-giggle stuff, but at that time there was absolutely no science to it. Pre-game practice sessions in the nets at the WACA Ground cost the association dearly—as one ball after another was wildly slogged over the fence. Match days were only vaguely different. Bowlers tried to find a defensive line and length, captains tried to set fields that were a compromise between attack and defence … and batsmen aimed to hit every ball out of the ground.

The World Series Cricket (WSC) days in 1978 and '79 finally presented a more strategic approach to one-day cricket. Captains and coaches began to study the precedents in this type of game, analysing and unearthing trends to improve their chances of success. The rules were also changed—for instance the number of players allowed in the deeps was limited—and this began to bite. Power plays were introduced, as were other changes, like coloured clothing, white balls and black sightscreens. The domestic Australian competition began with 40 overs a side, changing to the current 50 in 1978–79.

The expansion, worldwide, of limited-overs cricket over the years has developed a new breed of player: the short-form specialist. And with the advent of Twenty20 (T20) cricket—20 overs each side—it has been refined even further. I was coaching Kent in the English County competition when, in June 2003, the first formal competition in this format was staged. Playing at their new outground at Beckenham, Kent defeated Hampshire thanks to an amazing innings by Australian overseas professional Andrew Symonds. He reached 50 off 16 deliveries and was unbeaten on 96 from 37 balls. T20 had taken off with a big bang, which soon reverberated around the cricketing world.

Just look at David Warner—who played limited-overs games for Australia *before* he'd played first-class cricket (four-day games) for his state, New South Wales. Unheard-of stuff until the age of T20. A junior coach once told me he'd given up trying to teach straight-bat play to a highly talented lad in his squad, because the kid had told him, 'Not interested. I want to be like David Warner.'

But back to the WACA Ground in 1976. From its fairly humble beginnings in 1969, the Australian one-day competition had moved (but not all that far, to be honest) by the time Queensland and Western Australia shaped up against each other in the semifinal on 12 December. It was still basically a matter of hit out or get out, with 40 overs each to work with. And in those early days it is fair to say that there remained a bit of a lottery as to how the wicket would play. (A far cry from the batsman-friendly surfaces almost invariably turned out in latter days.) What neither side could begin to imagine, though, in the lead-up to this semifinal, was that the notorious WACA Ground strip would turn into a battlefield, with every delivery a potential hand grenade and each run as vital as any T20 run scored in the future.

Setting the scene

Let us set the scene for this Gillette Cup semifinal clash. It is generally held that the greatest, most traditional rivalry in Australian domestic cricket is between Victoria and New South Wales. And there's good reason for this—neighbouring states, two of the three original teams in the Sheffield Shield competition from its origin in 1892 (South Australia was the third), and their capital cities perennial rivals for the accolade of the business and cultural centres of the nation. However, since the other states' entry to the Sheffield Shield first-class cricket competition, a similarly robust rivalry has developed between Queensland and Western Australia.

Queensland had been admitted to the Shield competition in 1926, WA in 1947, and both Johnny-come-latelies were desperate to prove their worth on the big stage. In 1976, Queensland had yet to see their name inscribed on the trophy and the fact stuck in their collective craw. Western Australia, meanwhile, had taken the Shield in its very first season of entry (albeit on a part-time basis), and had gone on to win the trophy four more times over the ensuing years.

Fed up with the title of Australian cricket's 'easybeats', in the early 1970s the powers that were in Brisbane decided to up the ante. Previously, they'd recruited overseas stars—Tom Graveney (England), Majid Khan (Pakistan) and Alvin Kallicharran (West Indies)—to help weigh the cause in their favour. But without success. So, in 1973 they went to Australia's cricketing top and enticed Greg Chappell away from the South Australian team. This proved to be something of a turning point—bringing premium batting skills *and* a new captain with the potential to lead them out of the wilderness. The following season Jeff Thomson was lured north from New South Wales, and then the appeal of playing with Chappell and Thomson was too good to resist for Viv Richards, and he joined for the 1976–77 season. There were no excuses now.

If Queensland had struggled to get on the board in the Shield, it had fared slightly better in one-day cricket. In the second season of the domestic limited-overs tournament, WA and Queensland met in the final, which was ultimately won by WA. Two seasons later, Queensland was again runner-up, this time losing to New Zealand (playing in the competition by invitation for the first five seasons—and winning it three times). It was Queensland's turn in the final of 1975–76. In a remarkable clash at the Brisbane Cricket Ground (known as the Gabba) they defeated their old foes, WA, by just 4 runs. It was the state's first-ever trophy triumph.

Now, a season later, it was semifinals time and the stage was set for another cataclysmic clash between the two states. With three of the world's premier players in its line-up, Queensland had every reason to believe that the trophy was again there for the taking. First, though, they had to get through this game—against the dominant state team of the seventies with their own international stars, playing at home on a wicket unique in Australian cricket, and hungry for revenge after defeat at Queensland's hands in the final the year before.

The Miracle Match promised a lot! A virtual 'Who's Who' of world cricket at the time (and since) were warming up in the dressing rooms. While Queensland were lining up with Greg Chappell, Viv Richards and Jeff Thomson, WA included Rod Marsh as their captain, with the mercurial Dennis Lillee spearheading the bowling attack. The rest of the players who would soon walk onto the field also included a rising champ called Kim Hughes (for WA) plus nine other Test players of the future. The crowd of some 10,000 eager fans were on the edges of their seats. And they ended up getting more than they could ever have bargained for.

Lightning fast

It was enough to make the hair stand up on the back of your neck. Sitting in the members' stand at the WACA Ground, watching legendary West Indies (Windies) fast bowler Wes Hall, with the Fremantle Doctor (a south-westerly sea breeze that blew most afternoons at the WACA Ground) at his back, pounding in off a long run from the River End. And letting one fly so short that the batsman barely had to duck. Then watching the Windies wicketkeeper, Jerry Alexander, leaping to the sky, arm thrust out, trying to reach the soaring missile. He'd have needed a stepladder to reach it, and a tall one at that. Then straining forward in your seat to see the ball go one bounce into the boundary fence next to the sightscreen. Such was the nature of the surface of that wicket in November 1960. It had been rolled out like concrete, and big fellows like Wes could really make them fly.

As a result of performances like that, the WACA track had a reputation as the fastest and bounciest strip in the world. And curator Roy Abbott used to serve them up, time after time—encouraging one after another tearaway speedster to blossom out in the West. In my day, there were Ron Gaunt, Des Hoare, Graham McKenzie … and Dennis Lillee, with a heap of others not far behind. The pace and ferocity that could be produced on those 22 yards (20 metres) of fire and brimstone were unmatched, making it a truly dangerous track to bat on.

And remember, the 1970s was an era before batsmen could take comfort against fast bowlers on bouncy wickets behind the grille of a helmet. Before other protective accoutrements, like arm guards and chest guards, were introduced. All that most batsmen had were flimsy pads, gloves and protectors to save them from the hard leather of a cricket ball, potentially hurtling in at 160 kilometres an hour. As spectator and player I saw four players suffer a fractured jaw when hit facing quicks on the WACA track: Len Pavy (WA), Ray Jordon (Victoria), Bob Cunis (New Zealand) and Max Walker (Victoria). It was, at times, a truly vicious pitch.

All of which begs the question: Why the WACA Ground and not, say, the Adelaide Oval? Or Lord's, or Sabina Park, or Newlands? The answer is: it's all in the soil—the Harvey River soil, to be precise—that is used for the pitch. The Harvey River, some 100 kilometres south of Perth, formed over thousands of years, creating massive clay deposits when the river flooded and sedimentary overspill packed down to create a naturally hard surface. Smectite is the dominant clay in these soils and its properties ensure that it not only swells when wet and contracts when drying out, but sets particularly hard—guaranteeing the WACA Ground a history of a rock-hard, cracking pitch over the years.

Other crucial factors with turf wicket soils generally are the salts, and the calcium-to-magnesium ratio. You want pretty low salts, so you can grow grass. Magnesium tightens the soil up, while calcium helps relieve compaction. So, if you run two parts of calcium to one of magnesium, the wicket won't set as hard as it would with the ratios reversed. Roy Abbott appears to have run a very high magnesium and smectite soil on his pitches. As a result, the strip rolled out so hard that at times you could struggle to stand up on it in your spikes. For all intents and purposes the wicket at the WACA was like concrete—and hence produced that amazing bounce.

Grass in wickets needs time to recover after they've been rolled out and played on. In Roy Abbott's days this wasn't such a great issue, because there weren't that many playing days on the centre-wicket square. Perhaps it was used only twenty days a year, so he felt free to hammer the grass, knowing he'd have plenty of time to leave it fallow, so to speak. Today, recovery can be a problem, because you have to use each strip again and again through a season. Giving less chance for grass to recover.

The earliest recorded collection of the Harvey River soil for use on the WACA Ground pitch is 1938, but the practice no doubt started much earlier than that. Fortunately for the future of the fabled pitch, there is plenty of the black soil left on the banks of the Harvey River. The deposit runs as much as 200 metres out either side in the widest places, and up to a metre deep. Over the years, though, the grounds team have had to look beyond the bushland reserves of the Harvey River into farmlands, which, of course, have been treated differently. The clay soil there has been ploughed, it's had fertilisers and chemicals poured into it, it's had crops on it and it's had cattle prancing up and down over it. And all this tends to change the soil structure. Those harvesting the precious material usually cream off only the top 20 to 30 cm. And the soil is then sent off for analysis, to ensure the quality remains.

Frozen butter

Now we understand a bit more about the nature of the soil that forms the WACA Ground strip, what was it about that pitch on 12 December 1976 that changed it from one of the most notorious in the world into such a demon? On which batsmen were forced to play Russian roulette just to survive?

Roy Abbott's normal preparation of a wicket for, say, a Sheffield Shield game starting on a Friday would probably have included the following. He'd have looked to have it pretty wet on the Monday morning, to muddy it up, roll it a bit, and then water it back in on Monday night. Then Tuesday, Wednesday and Thursday, plenty more rolling to prepare the surface. Plus, depending on the weather, an occasional spray of water to keep the surface 'alive'. Hot and dry—some water. Cool and wet—no water. That's a process of four days.

For a one-day match he probably would have started preparation five days out, so the game would be played on a surface similar to the second day of a Shield game. Historically on that strip, day two would provide the best batting conditions—predictable bounce with cracks yet to appear. Sadly, we can't ask the man what happened that week in December all those years ago. We can only surmise that he either had problems with the weather and the clay was soft right through the profile, or he decided to give it a drink a day out and it made it uncommonly soft on top. What we do know is that it's a really difficult clay to manage. If you get it wrong either way—without moisture or with moisture—it either cracks or it swells a bit. Cracks provide variable and unpredictable bounce, the alternative being steepling bounce and movement off the seam. One or the other, on the fastest pitch in the world, that can become dangerous.

When the two captains cast their eyes down on the green and shiny surface that Sunday they would have seen a pitch promising steepling bounce—very uncomfortable for the batsmen, and a birthday for the pacemen. Chappell relished the challenge. Not only did he have the thunderbolts of Jeff Thomson at his beck and call, but he also had Viv Richards to open the batting and himself at number four to master the deliveries from WA. Okay, his opponents would have Dennis Lillee, plus a handy batting line-up, but if Queensland could prove they had a stronger arsenal to conquer these conditions they would surely win the day.

Here are the first impressions from some of the key players.

Greg Chappell: When I first saw the track I thought 'Bloody hell—this would be a challenge for a Test match, but for a one-dayer it will be very interesting.'

Rod Marsh: It was one of those pitches that was very dark, with not a lot of grass on it. But that's what WACA pitches were like then on day one. It was probably going to do a bit.

John Maclean: I described the wicket as frozen butter— it was hard, but it had a sort of slippery surface. That meant that Jeff Thomson's deliveries were inclined to slide through off the surface, rather than bite and move off the seam.

Viv Richards: It wasn't necessarily naughty. If you were familiar with the nature of the WACA Ground pitch you would know that there would always be plenty of bounce.

Bruce Yardley: It was not a great one-day pitch. There was moisture and grass, and a one-day pitch is supposed to be the same throughout the day, which it wasn't.

Phil Carlson: It was a greasy greentop. Because of the excessive movement—through the air and off the wicket—you had to bowl very well to be effective. With the movement off the seam, it would either keep on going the way of the swing, or cut back the other way.

We'll never know the reason for the track being the way it was on 12 December 1976. But what we do know is that, in his own way, the man who made it played a very real role in this extraordinary game.

Heads or tails?

The sun was shining down on the WACA Ground, and a healthy crowd was building up, when opposing captains Greg Chappell and Rod Marsh stood on the pitch for the coin toss. Each would, figuratively at least, have had fingers crossed behind his back for good luck with the fall of the coin. Both would have sensed that the outcome of the toss could almost decide the outcome of the game.

Greg Chappell: No question we would bowl if I won the toss. And I expected that with our attack on that track we would bowl them out for a gettable total.

Rod Marsh: It was a toss you were almost happy to lose. These were relatively early days in one-day cricket and at that time you were never quite certain whether to bat first … but I think we'd have been happy to bowl first.

All the Queensland captain's wishes came true. He had no hesitation in ordering WA to bat.

With his potential trump card, Jeff Thomson, eagerly measuring out his run at the River End of the ground and a menacing-looking pitch, Greg Chappell would have been excused for being exuberant at the commencement of the first innings. For the Western Australian opening batsmen, Bruce Laird and Ric Charlesworth, the situation couldn't have been more different. Facing Thomson on any sort of wicket—not necessarily even with a new cherry in his hand—was always going to be a colossal task, but with the WACA pitch smooth and gleaming, the odds were stacked against them. The conditions totally favoured the fast bowler—limited-overs cricket wasn't supposed to be like this!

> Ric Charlesworth: The wicket looked green to me and this was confirmed when I marked my guard. When you pulled your spike through to make the mark it was almost slippery. I don't know how this could have happened. Facing Thommo downwind with a new ball was a daunting prospect at the best of times, but this was something different.

> Bruce Laird: The wicket was a bit wet. Oily, like the old WACA Ground wickets on the first day of a Shield game. This day, when you scratched your guard down with a spike, it came away moist. Didn't have that white look to it, like the best WACA one-day wickets.

Both batsmen were renowned for their courage in the face of fire against true pace bowling. On this day, they would need all of that—and more. Sitting in the relative comfort of the dressing room, their teammates crossed their fingers that they might come out of the ordeal unscathed as they watched Thomson standing at the top of his mark.

Stumpy and Grumpy

Bruce Laird and
Ric Charlesworth

Laird

World Series Cricket (WSC) may still be viewed by some in a rather jaundiced light, but it *was* a revolution … in the truest sense. It brought to cricket night play under lights—and with it white balls, black sightscreens and coloured clothing, plus drop-in pitches, fielding circles, brilliant multi-camera television coverage and a much bigger slice of the money cake for the players. And it was the platform on which Australian opening batsman Bruce Laird showed his very best stuff. Laird was a five-year veteran for WA when he was signed for WSC, and had already proven his stomach for facing fast bowlers with the new ball in their hands. Those who picked the Australian squad for WSC recognised he'd need all of that against speedsters of the calibre of Michael Holding,

Andy Roberts, Colin Croft, Mike Procter, Garth Le Roux and Imran Khan.

WSC began in 1977–78 with six Supertests for Australia—three against the West Indies and three against a World XI. Laird played four games and scored two centuries against high-quality bowling. Standing at a mere 172 centimetres, Bruce 'Stumpy' Laird's short stature may have been a bit of a plus, when the trend was to bang the ball in halfway down the wicket at batsmen. Against this stuff, courage was required. Protective gear was rudimentary, and if you got in behind the ball the odds were you'd be hit now and then. Laird was one who never failed to get in behind the next one. In fact, he once told me he'd much prefer to face these speedsters, one after another, than sit in close at short leg when power hitter Gordon Greenidge was on strike—the burly West Indian opener was big on whacking the ball off his pads. Laird figured the reaction time from Greenidge's bat to him 3 metres away was much less than the time a Holding flier took to reach him standing on the popping crease!

Laird struggled in the home series in WSC's second season, but remained in the side for a tour to the West Indies. Thank goodness, because in the third Supertest at Trinidad he played one of the great innings of its type. Batting first, Australia slumped to 5–32. Laird stuck his chin out, took a battering, and his masterly 122 saw his side to what had seemed an unlikely total of 246—enough to go on and win the game. At the close of play on that first day, the Australians trooped in to the West Indies dressing room for some camaraderie. Captain Ian Chappell found himself sitting next to the quality Windies opening bat, Roy Fredericks. In their conversation, a royal salute—'Tell Bruce,' Freddo said, 'that I wish I'd played that innings today.'

When the pundits looked back on the WSC years and composed their best team from all those who played, many had Laird opening the batting with the incomparable Barry Richards. High, high praise. And Windies captain Clive Lloyd, when asked if there was an Australian player he would have welcomed in any of the teams he led, replied, 'Yes. Bruce Laird.' The little fellow's sheer guts appealed to us all.

For Laird, it had been a long haul to the top of international cricket. Having begun with WA in 1973, he was twenty-nine when he finally made his Test debut at the Gabba in 1979, picking his way through the West Indies attack of Andy Roberts, Michael Holding, Colin Croft and Joel Garner to reach 92 before falling in fading light. It was an innings characterised by dogged defence and occasional attack. There weren't too many half volleys from that speed quartet! He followed up with 75 in the second innings and two more half-centuries in the three-Test series. Strangely, though, in twenty-one Tests he never posted a three-figure score. Possessed of a good technique and an even better temperament, Laird was recognised as the bravest of the brave. It is hard all these years on to remember his favourite stroke. Maybe it was the glide to leg off his pads. But as one who batted behind him in the order for club and state, *my* favourite Laird shot was back and across to take the ball high on the bat and drop it at his feet.

Bruce Laird was—still is, as a matter of fact—a man of few words. And, such is the degree of his modesty, that you'd never know he'd done anything more outstanding than catch a herring off the rocks. But those who knew him well, teammates and opponents alike, would all say that above being one of the great Aussie battlers with bat in hand he is a really good bloke.

Charlesworth

As a nation, Australians have shown a real penchant for giving people nicknames, and even prime ministers can't escape the custom—Robert Menzies was dubbed by his opponents as 'Pig Iron Bob'. In the country's sports teams, the practice is followed almost religiously, and if you don't have one there must be something wrong with you—it's almost a badge of honour. Extrapolate that to cricket, a game where players spend so much time together in a fusty dressing room while their mates are out in the middle batting, and it's no wonder so many nicknames are contrived—and of such a wide variety. Some are clever. For instance, enigmatic New South Wales spinner John Gleeson copped 'CHO' because of his tendency to vanish from the dressing room soon after play had ended for the day—'cricket hours only'. Some were less than flattering. For instance, WA pace bowler Wayne Clark was called 'Dunny'—his initials and the Aussie vernacular for a toilet just seemed to add up.

Others were more personal and, sometimes, a little more hurtful. As an opening batting pair, the WA duo were bound together by rhyming nicknames—the small-statured Bruce 'Stumpy' Laird's similarly short opening partner, Ric Charlesworth, was given 'Grumpy' from the get-go. This, of course, was inspired by the band of mostly rhyming-named dwarfs in the Snow White story. However, taking the lustre off what must have seemed like a good idea at the time (or adding more schoolyard shine, depending on their attitude) is the fact that Ric Charlesworth had a brother who was born with dwarfism.

Fortunately, though, for those of us who subscribed to the moniker, Grumpy was never grumpy. In fact, he was a very happy chappy. His round face was dominated by sparkling eyes and a wonderful smile that revealed the most amazing set of teeth. And for that, Grumpy had given his dentist father a nickname of his own: 'The Molar Marauder'. And behind Grumpy's broad smile is an incredible brain. In fact, his list of accomplishments, both in and out of sport, makes him one of the most extraordinary people, and great achievers, I've ever met.

Ric Charlesworth followed in the footsteps of his father, Lester Charlesworth, who played eight first-class games for WA between 1949 and 1951. Like father, like son—both were left-hand bats, both scored a century for the state, and both averaged just over 30. I can't say much about Lester's game, but to my mind Ric's only shortcoming was that he placed too many limitations on his stroke play. He was as solid as a rock and as courageous as his mate Stumpy, but there were shots I'd see him play at club level that *never* saw the light of day on the bigger stage.

That said, I can understand how he might not have reached his full potential as a batsman. For most of his days playing for WA (1972–80) he had other things on his plate as well. Big things. Like being voted the best hockey player in the world. Like studying and working towards being a doctor. At one stage the latter pursuit was making serious inroads to his cricket. He was working nights, doing his internship at a Perth hospital, and more than once we would arrive in the dressing room on the morning of a game for WA to find him lying on the rubdown table, catching up on some sleep.

In 1983, with cricket- and hockey-playing behind him, Charlesworth was elected a federal politician. After ten years in Parliament he moved straight into coaching, guiding the Australian women's hockey team to Olympic gold at Atlanta (1996) and Sydney (2000). He has since been appointed a Master Coach by the International Hockey Federation and is regularly described as one of the world's best coaches … in any sport. Ever curious and prepared to learn, he shifted tack in 2001 and took on an assistant coaching role with the Australian Rules football club Fremantle, before spending two years working as High Performance Manager of New Zealand cricket. More recently his remarkable career in coaching took him back to base—as the successful coach of the Australian men's hockey team.

Ric Charlesworth may have been a limited stroke player, but nobody ever questioned his courage against the quicks. And in his time there were a few good ones around. His ability to blunt those bullying brutes was a major contribution to several successful years for his state.

Slingshot superstar

Jeff Thomson

What a lowdown con trick! This bloke comes lolloping in on a pretty short approach, completely casual. As a batsman at the other end you begin to think you might get on the front foot and spank anything that's even half fullish in length. The deception continues as he throws his back leg out to his left and turns into the delivery stride. It's one of those movements that isn't quite fluid. Legs look as though they could get tangled up—and he might even fall over. But then all hell breaks loose. From the most perfect side-on position he releases a lightning bolt. The batsman braces and waits in hope—that he might just get a bat on it, or that it might miss him and fire through to the 'keeper, who's standing halfway to the boundary!

Yes. Jeff Thomson with ball in hand was a *real* handful. At his blistering pace they worked out you had something like 0.43 of a second to react. Then those same people tell you it's actually impossible for a human being to react in such a short space of time. So, how did batsmen cope—in times before helmets were worn to protect the head and offer some sort of solace?

John Inverarity, who pretty well throughout his career for Western Australia batted at the fall of the first wicket, came up with a plan. As Thommo's back leg was moving to the plant position in the delivery stride—and the ball was hidden down behind his right buttock, about to begin a very long arc to release—you started moving. Back and across. Bat raised. And hopeful. Gave you just that bit more reaction time.

In December 1975, boffins from the University of Western Australia took some high-tech camera gear to the WACA Ground, to clock the fast bowling line-ups during the Second Test between Australia and the West Indies. Included in their sights were Andy Roberts, Michael Holding, Dennis Lillee … and Thommo. And while the other fast bowlers *were* fast, compared to Thomson their deliveries were little more than medium-pacers. Dennis Lillee's best, for example, tracked at 86.4 mph (139.01 kph), while slingshot Thommo came in at 99.7 mph (160.39 kph). Clearly a rung above.

Clive Lloyd, who captained the deadliest pace barrage the West Indies ever produced, calls Thomson 'the quickest I have seen. As quick on the first ball of the day as he was at 5 pm. There was no respite.' Viv Richards agrees. 'He was definitely the fastest bowler I ever faced. At his speed you just had no time to react.'

Speaking to Thommo about those times, his intense blue eyes tend to glaze over.

I'm told Clive Lloyd said that Barbados 1978 was the fastest new-ball bowling he had ever seen—and I guess in his own sides he'd been pretty close to a few of the fastest. But I don't think it was my quickest. The days I bowled really fast, I never quite realised it was happening. They were the days when you were in fourth gear and you realised you still had another gear to go. It's like everything's in slow motion.

In one particular game, a Shield game in Brisbane against Victoria in March 1975, Thomson definitely found that fifth gear.

When we batted I made 61 runs, just belted them around. I was thinking 'This is my day.' When I went out to bowl they just came out beautifully. Ask Ian Redpath—Redders was a pretty good bat and he had no idea. It helped that the boys in the slips took everything that came their way. In that innings I got 6 wickets for not that many. [6 for 17 from 12.6 overs, in fact. Including Redpath and two others in one over]. Then there was Adelaide against the Pakistanis ... I bowled really, really quick that day. I had a couple of wickets before lunch, but the Pakistani batsmen had no idea. That day could have been anything.

Of all people, Queensland's 'keeper, John Maclean, knew about Thommo's pace.

I recall two times for Queensland when he really let rip. In Brisbane against Victoria, late in the afternoon he was so fast that for them it was seriously protection of your life. Another day in Sydney, they were five for 160-odd. Phil Carlson was fielding at mid-off and Thommo said to him on the way back to his mark, 'How are they coming out?' Something had got him fired up—and I'm going back about a metre every ball. Then he started tailing the ball in and he cleaned them up for less than 200. He talked about 'blood on the pitch' … well it was lucky there was none that day.

Rod Marsh: Keeping to him was really good fun. He wasn't as accurate as Dennis and you had to do a lot of work back there … but you were a long way back, so you had enough time to move your feet.

From the batsman's point of view, Greg Chappell:

Thommo was far and away the fastest bowler I ever saw. Probably the best natural athlete, too. He was born to run fast, bowl fast, throw hard, drive fast—he did everything at 100 miles an hour! Just a natural person, too. In a newspaper interview one day he told the journalist who'd asked him about how he bowled, 'Mate, I just shuffle up and go *wang*.' And that's what he did.

Kim Hughes: Thommo was the quickest I ever faced. He was as far ahead in terms of speed as Bradman was ahead of the rest as a batsman. At his fastest he would have been around 170 … these days they're lucky to get to 150. One day in the mid-seventies at the WACA Ground, John Maclean was standing so far back you'd have been excused for thinking he was in another game!

So how did this phenomenal speed come about?

Physically, Jeff Thomson was magnificent. Cut like a park statue. Then there was his unusual action. And, to execute the latter you needed plenty of the former. Thommo says the secret of his speed and bounce was 'all in the load-up—getting very tall through the crease and bowling over a braced front leg'. As simple as that? Maybe. As fast bowlers go, Thommo was of medium height, but there was power plus in his musculature. The power came from muscles in the back, which helped propel the ball with a type of catapult action. To see Thommo from behind in a T-shirt was to witness an amazing triangular shape: broad shoulders, massive back muscles, tapering down to a narrow waist.

Thomson, himself, had this matter-of-fact insight to explain his natural strength:

> As a young bloke I worked on the wharves and used to load wool bales. I'd pick 'em up and stack 'em, ready for the carrier to come and take them. At other times I'd load a couple of hundred 18 gallon [80 litre] kegs in a day, picking up a full one on my own. That gave me strong guts and a strong back. I never broke down.

And this to add about his leg development:

> I used to play professional soccer and you used to run all day. You got the best legs ever, racing up and down. I didn't mean it that way. It's just that what I did helped make me what I was.

Naturally, his new-ball partner, Dennis Lillee, was a great admirer:

> Thommo was a marvellous natural athlete … totally gifted in everything he did. And a brilliant physical specimen. Big arms and chest and huge back muscles, which he needed to pull him through his action. Amazing athlete's legs, like a sprinter at the Olympics. He was a terrifying prospect for any batsman. Off that jaunting bit of a run-up he wound up so much pace. Add to that the fact that the ball seemed to come up sharply off a length more than it did for anybody else. Because he was so quick, he could afford to pitch a bit fuller and still the ball would rear up.

Viv Richards agrees:

> When he found that length—basically just short of a good length—he was as good as it gets. He had so much power and energy in his action. The amount of wickets he took with balls lifting sharply off that good length was amazing. He was very, very special you know.

So, the combination of an unusual action, extraordinary musculature and power *and* a degree of diffidence and devil-may-care. The action came from his father before him. 'He never tried to teach me to bowl that way, just as I never tried to influence my son, Matt, who also has the same action.' It just happened. A gifted youth, his casual approach would drive many a coach and captain to distraction. As teenagers from Sydney's working-class western suburbs, he and his mate Lennie Pascoe (himself a talented fast bowler who would play for New South Wales and Australia) grew to love the surf. And the girls down on the beach. Fishing was another serious attraction. If the mood of the day took the two off in one of those directions, then the mundane matter of attending a practice session—even arriving on time for the start of a game—went flying out the window. They would think nothing of turning up in board shorts and thongs, surfboards on the roof rack:

> It didn't affect our cricket. We'd still bowl flat out for Bankstown. But we'd roll up late for a game occasionally—and we'd get into trouble. The spinners would be on and the captain would be very unhappy.

Despite his casual approach, Thommo was committed to having a go at cricket, and in the 1972–73 season he was selected to play for New South Wales in the opening game. He was twenty-two years of age.

The game was against Queensland in Brisbane. The Blues batted first, but it rained for most of the first two days. New captain John Benaud could tell Thommo was becoming more tense as time went by, sitting around the dressing room and the team motel. In the end Benaud told him to go out and have a few beers. Which he enthusiastically proceeded to do. The next day Thomson was hung-over when play finally got underway, but he still managed to claim a couple of wickets and the game ended in a draw.

Next up was playing WA in Perth, where Jeff Thomson met Dennis Lillee for the first time. Thommo ignored his teammates' plea not to bounce Lillee and got one up to strike him on the gloves. As the West Australian ran by it led to this exchange. Lillee: 'I hope you can hold a bat, pal.' Thommo: 'Listen pal, you've got the bat at the moment … get up the other end and see how good you are.' They were the only words in anger the pair would ever share.

Thommo was chosen to make his international debut that same season, against Pakistan in the Second Test at the MCG. This offered the chance to team up *with* Dennis Lillee, for whom he'd already formed a high degree of respect. Thomson, though, was so keen to play that he went into the game with a foot injury. 'The foot just gave out and I couldn't even walk back to the team hotel [little more than a kilometre away] at the end of play.'

Thomson bowled just 2 overs in Pakistan's second innings, for match figures of 19 overs, 0–110. It turned out he had a broken bone in a foot and missed the rest of the season. This led to bitter disappointment and frustration for Thomson, which was compounded the following season when the NSW selectors bypassed him. As the summer wore on thoughts of a move interstate took root. With South Australia in mind.

In the meantime, he continued to tear into club sides and had stumps flying in all directions. And finally the NSW selectors paid attention. He was chosen for the last game of the season, against Queensland at the Sydney Cricket Ground (SCG). Queensland needed to win the game to claim the Sheffield Shield for the first time. They won the toss and put NSW in first.

When it was their turn to bat, they met Thommo on a mission. He blitzed the Queenslanders to the tune of 7–85— including Greg Chappell, who decided then and there it would be far better to have Thommo on his team than ever again have to face him in anger. After the game, which Queensland lost, Greg approached Thommo over a beer—and found great interest in a move across the border. The rest is history.

It was July 1974 when Thomson packed his bags and headed to his new home. He got a job working as a car salesman and set about getting ready to bowl fast for his new state. Greg Chappell, delighted to have him on side, said at the time:

> I don't care if Thommo hasn't a clue where they are going. He'll frighten these blokes out. They'll be so desperate to get to the other end they'll run themselves out.

Later that year the move paid off and he was chosen again to play for Australia. It was the First Test against England at the Gabba in November 1974. Says Thommo, 'I was ready to go, super fit and bowling the fastest of my life.' He and Dennis Lillee proceeded to knock the England bats back on their heels, thus beginning a short period of utter dominance by the pair—and Australia. The visitors compounded. Dismissed for 265, despite a brave and provocative century by Tony Greig. Thommo's figures: 3–59. In the second innings there was mayhem. This time Greig succumbed to the 'sandshoe crusher', a yorker that hit him on the foot and cannoned into his leg stump. Thomson added 6–46, for match figures of 9–105.

Lillee was full of praise at the fireworks. 'You could see their whole being was in survival mode.' That set the tone. Australia won the six-Test series 4–1. Between them, Thomson (who was injured playing tennis on the rest day of the Fifth Test and didn't play in the Sixth) and Lillee (who bowled only 6 overs in the Sixth) claimed 58 wickets. Thommo landed 33 of them, at

17.93 apiece. Keith Miller, no slouch himself in his day with the new ball, wrote from the safety of the press box in Brisbane, 'He frightened me, and I was sitting 200 yards [180 metres] away.'

There was more of the same when the West Indies toured Australia the following summer. This time the six-Test series was won 5–1, and the twins of terror bagged 56 between them (though Lillee missed the Fourth Test with a chest infection). Thommo took 29 wickets in the six Tests. It was a dream come true for Australia. But it turned into a nightmare for Thomson at the Adelaide Oval the next season (1976–77) against Pakistan.

It was the First Test and on Christmas Eve, of all days, Thomson was bowling with his usual wonderful rhythm and pace—bombing the great Pakistani Zaheer Abbas and making them fly on a typical easy-paced Adelaide track. Then, upset that mid-wicket fieldsman Alan Turner had missed two opportunities to take a catch, when a third chance came Thomson made a fateful decision—not to let Turner fluff this one, too. He dashed across to complete the catch himself and the pair collided. Ligaments were torn away from Thommo's right shoulder and he required immediate surgery, and a rehab program. 'People said I would never play again, but I was determined to get back to my full playing strength.' He missed the remainder of the season, but set out to work harder than he ever had to get back to fitness.

> Greg Chappell: Hardly a worse thing could have happened for Australian cricket. For two and a half home seasons of Test cricket he'd been phenomenal. Thommo was reduced by maybe as much as 30 per cent after that. He could still bowl quick, but he had to run in hard and put a lot more effort into it. He didn't have the elasticity and he didn't have the strength.

There was no way Thomson would regain fitness in time for the ill-fated 1977 tour to England (blighted by the undercurrents of the formation of World Series Cricket). Thommo signed for the rebel outfit, but was forced to withdraw through the terms of a contract with Brisbane radio station 4IP. He returned to play a one-day game and five Sheffield Shield games for the Maroons in 1977–78. Later he indicated a desire to join his old teammates at WSC. A court challenge, funded by WSC, resulted in a rare victory at the time for the Australian Cricket Board (ACB). A miffed Thomson played just one limited-overs game for Queensland in 1978–79 (returning the stunning figures of 6–18), then sat out the rest of the season.

Finally, as part of the terms of a peace treaty, the ACB agreed to let him play in the last hurrah of the rebel group, a tour to the West Indies. Reunited with Lillee, he took 16 wickets in five Supertests, with a best of 5–78 at Trinidad. Thommo loved being back with his mates. 'Boy did I enjoy this series. It was the toughest cricket of my life. War on the cricket field.' However, as much as he had loved the experience, he would later reject an offer to play for the rebel Australian sides in South Africa. The plain truth of the matter is, Thommo was never quite the same after that horrendous collision at the Adelaide Oval.

Together Jeff Thomson and Dennis Lillee formed one of the most formidable—and intimidating—new-ball attacks in the long history of the game. Referred to as the 'Lillian Thomson' duet, from the mid-seventies they rode roughshod over the best the rest of the world could offer. Part of the secret of their combined success may have been the fact they were so different from each other.

They certainly had contrasting actions. Lillee of the long, energetic, mesmerising run, the long leap, during which he turned into a rocked-back side-on position on landing, the vigorous follow-through, the menacing scamper down the wicket after delivery getting into the batsman's space and the fabled Lillee 'glare'. Thommo of the short, ambling approach, the tangle-footed turn, from virtually no leap into the side-on position, the javelin thrower's heave through the delivery stride and the almost-apologetic easing-up a few steps down the track.

And contrasting temperaments. Lillee of the firebrand aggression and will to dominate, from first ball to last in a day's play. Thommo of the laid-back, just-get-the-job-done nature, who almost needed something—or somebody—to turn up the flames.

Lillee describes Thomson in those days as a man of few words:

> ... almost an introvert. We often roomed together and yet we'd never talk about cricket. Not once. Not about bowling, or about batsmen. I used to think about these things a lot, but with Thommo it was all gut instinct. Out in the middle he would have a go at himself a fair bit, but otherwise he had little to say. Certainly, I can't remember him having any confrontations with batsmen. He'd just bowl and go back to his mark and bowl again. A bit like Graham McKenzie before him.

Thommo is quoted as having said, 'I enjoy hitting the batsman more than getting him out. I like to see blood on the pitch.' These days he doubts he actually said that.

But his partner, Lillee, makes no bones about what he said back then. 'I try and hit a batsman in the ribcage when I bowl a purposeful bouncer—and I want it to hurt so much that he doesn't want to face me any more.' Yes, believe it or not, in many ways Thommo was a retiring personality. Until he got worked up, of course.

Dennis Lillee will never forget the days when he and his mate wrought havoc:

> I always felt that if I wasn't getting wickets, he would. He says he felt the same about me. I guess we made a good team within a team. It was like, 'if I don't get a wicket now, I might not get any'—it sort of spurred you on, as well. It was almost like you expected something to happen all the time. There were days when he just bowled like the wind, when I'd be inclined to think my role might be to just keep it tight and let's do the attacking from his end. It's not that you weren't trying, more that you could see that he was having a day out and your job was more to play a support role.

Ashes to Ashes, dust to dust … if Lillee don't get ya, Thommo must.

In 1979, the Australian Cricket Board, affected by the 'rebel' WSC, assembled a team of players under captain Bob Simpson (back from retirement) to tour the West Indies. The ACB's tough stand on the rebel group meant that the team selected wasn't even of 'second eleven' standing, although Thomson was part of it. The local authorities in the Caribbean weren't so offended by the advent of WSC, though, and immediately chose a full-strength side.

During the First Test at Trinidad, Roberts, Croft and Garner cleaned up the visitors and the West Indies won by an innings and 106 runs. This terrible imbalance continued into the Second Test at Barbados. Again the battered and bruised Australians had to face up to the terrifying trio. Thommo, vice-captain of the Australian team, decided enough was enough. 'They had belted us in the First Test and there we were at Barbados, copping it again. I decided to have a real crack at them.'

Three men who played for WA in 'The Miracle Match' were in the Australian team at Barbados on that memorable day—Bruce Yardley, Craig Serjeant and Wayne Clark.

> Clark: Thommo went out to make a statement. It was as though he wanted to kill someone. A contest between gladiators … no holding back on either side. Fielding down at fine leg, I could gauge the crowd's reaction. They just loved fast bowling—and they loved what they were seeing: the fastest bowler in the world against the world's best batsmen. Those batsmen were jumping around a bit, too, but that didn't mean they were scared. Just tells you how quick he was bowling.

If Jeff Thomson needed an excuse—any excuse—to get really wound up, it came in his first over:

> It all started for me when I was bowling at Gordon Greenidge, who never made many runs against me and Dennis. I got one to fly on him and he gloved it to gully, who caught it. It was clearly out, but Gordon stayed and the umpire was unmoved by our appeal. He rubbed his shoulder, but I'll bet he was dying to rub his hand, too, it must have been hurting so much. I was really pissed

off and said, 'Right, if that's how you want to play it, look out!' I just cranked it right up.

Shortly after that Greenidge fell to Thommo ... and in came Richards. Game on!

> Thomson: A confrontation with Viv was looming. When you're fired up and he is, too, it's something like a shootout. You keep slugging away and he keeps counterpunching. I found that when playing in Tests against him ... it was a question of who was going to break first.

> Bruce Yardley: It was clear that Viv thought the only way forward would be to go on an all-out attack. It was do or die. A showdown between two great players. Thommo really let go.

Immediately, the West Indian was hammered on the left pad and hobbled around before facing up again.

> Serjeant: The second ball that Thommo bowled to Viv was the quickest ball I've ever seen. It was short and Viv was really late to duck and get out of the way. He didn't have a helmet and we just knew that he was rattled.

Then Richards went the favoured pull shot. But the ball got big on him and he spooned it to backward square leg. Trevor Laughlin spilled a difficult chance—a life for Richards on nought, and Thommo far from impressed.

> I could have run around and caught it myself, it hung up there for so long. I've done my quince and shouted, 'What the fuck do you think this is, it's not as though we can afford to give any chances!'

The drama continued. Richards hit on the glove by a steepling flier. The atmosphere by now electric. Two of the very best 'bulls' of the game locking horns. Thommo enjoying himself *and* the bouncy track. He bounced Richards again. 'I really let this one go and he pulled it off his nose.' The result was a flat-batted pull that went screaming through mid-wicket and crashed into a corrugated iron roof beyond the boundary, then careered out of the ground. Both bowler and batsman looked at each other in amazement. All of the bowler's strength had gone into the delivery and all of the batsman's power had gone into the shot. It flew past not that far from Yardley, who barely saw a blur. As they went looking for the ball, Yardley stood, transfixed.

> I said to myself 'Yes! This is Test cricket at its highest level.' The ball went out of the ground and there was a delay while it was retrieved, but I was just looking at Viv and thinking 'How good is that!'

Richards remained on the hunt. A few balls later he laid back and slogged a fuller-pitched delivery back over Thomson's head for four. Thommo also remained on the prowl.

> Next ball left him outside off and he played and missed. As I walked back I thought, 'Fuck this, I'm going high again!' I put everything into it, the ball got up around his nose, he went for it, he was cramped for room and he skied it to fine leg.

… Where Wayne Clark faced the task of taking the catch. It was a stop-start affair—would he or wouldn't he get there. 'It was coming down really high and in the end I misjudged it and had to dive forward to secure it.' Clark came up with dirt in his fingernails. As Richards trundled off with 23 next to his name, Clark was embraced by the whole Australian team.

But the perpetrator of this highest degree of sporting drama was Jeffrey Robert Thomson. He took 3 wickets from 6.5 of the most hostile overs imaginable that evening—and ended with innings figures of 6–77. One up for the man they called 'Two-Up' (named after Thommo's two-up school in Sydney).

Though no great shakes with the bat in hand, Thommo had a few days to remember at the crease. None better than the final day of the Melbourne Test against England in 1982–83. When he walked out to join the redoubtable Allan Border late on day four, Australia was 9–218 chasing 292 for victory—as good as all over. The pair survived to stumps and the authorities declared free entry the following morning. Why not? One wicket to fall and 37 runs still needed. Some 10,000 loyal Victorian fans were on hand for the start of play, a number that continued to swell to 18,000 through the morning.

Whenever Thommo got bat on ball the crowd roared. The chase went on and they'd been out there for 17 overs when, with 4 runs needed for the most unlikely of victories, Ian Botham took up the attack. Botham got one to climb on Thommo, who flashed at it and edged it to Chris Tavare at first slip. Tavare, though, could only knock it up—and it was caught behind him by second slip, Geoff Miller. A wonderful run chase had fallen tantalisingly close. Thommo's contribution: 21, out of a stand worth 70.

The 1985 tour to England was Thommo's swan song for Australia. He played in the First and Fifth Tests and his 3 wickets meant he'd retire on exactly 200 from a rather tormented 51-Test career. He chose to play on for Queensland in 1985–86 and suffered the disappointment of failing to win the Shield final, against New South Wales in Sydney. Then he retired and went to his family. From there he tried his hand at coaching, leading Queensland for five years in the early 1990s. And keeping himself busy on the side, fast driving, water skiing (flat out), fishing and hunting razorbacks. He took up a family love of plants and began a landscape gardening business, and for a while he ran a fishing-boat charter business.

These days it's the speaking circuit and a game of golf here and there. You sense here is a man who ran the good race and now lives with no regrets.

Let play begin

As Bruce Laird etched the first mark to be made on the black-and-green strip, dead on ten o'clock in the morning, the broad shoulders of Jeff Thomson loomed large away in the distance at the southern end, or River End, of the ground. Seemingly impervious to the importance of the moment, the laconic Queensland opener rolled through his action a couple of times to Denis Schuller, standing a few metres away at mid-on. T-shirts and shorts were de rigueur for the swelling crowd—and high up in the Channel Nine commentary box were four former Australian captains—Richie Benaud, Bill Lawry, Bob Simpson and Ian Chappell. They and the fans shared the anticipation of fireworks that the short form normally provided. But none had any inkling of the mayhem that was to follow.

Perhaps now is a good time to remind ourselves of the rules under which this game would be played. There would be an allocation of 40 eight-ball overs for each side, with no bowler permitted to bowl more than eight. In those early days of limited-overs cricket, there was no limit to the number of bouncers to be bowled in an over. The only tool in the umpires' box in this regard was their ability to act on the wording 'intimidatory play'. Plus, there was no such thing as a leg-side wide, and there were no restrictions in field placings.

But Thommo—any day, anywhere—before the shoulder injury he was to suffer later that month, was a fearsome prospect. And, at twenty-six years of age, he was in the prime period of his career. Faster than ever, but with gathering degrees of control the more he bowled. In Laird and Ric Charlesworth, WA had two robust competitors. A right-hander and a left-hander. But both knew the size of the task that lay ahead of them in conditions clearly favouring their wild and woolly opponent.

While batsmen at the time had very little to offer in the form of protective gear, Charlesworth had something rather different—he'd picked up on an early type of skullcap that had been quietly introduced by the England captain, Mike Brearley, a forerunner of the now-universal batsman's helmet. It was made of a skin-coloured, dense plastic material, moulded to the shape of the individual's skull, with extensions down over the vulnerable temple area. Grumpy had the skullcap stitched inside a white floppy hat and it would have given him a little added confidence as he watched from the non-striker's end as Thommo got ready to let fly.

At the striker's end, Laird sized up the conditions:

> It looked like it was going to do a bit—and it did. There was a lot of swing and plenty of movement off the deck. Everything was in the seam bowlers' favour, though I think Thommo slipped on the first ball—in fact, I don't think he ever felt fully free to let it rip.

Clearly Thomson was having his problems. His interrupted foot plant meant that he was slightly down on his menacing pace, and his accuracy, vital in such favourable circumstances, was astray. Manna from heaven for the two batsmen. As Charlesworth put it, 'Fortunately Thommo was having trouble standing up through his delivery stride.' Still, he was making the ball fly through to the 'keeper ... some pace and plenty of bounce ... occasionally beating the outside edge of the WA bats.

After an erratic start, with the final ball of his second over Thomson sent one down well up and wide outside Laird's off stump. Looking to flay the ball away off the back foot, Laird took a thick outside edge and was caught by Ogilvie in the gully.

> Richie Benaud: That went like a rocket—came right off the meat of the bat and Ogilvie plucked it out of thin air—a brilliant piece of fielding.

WA 1–8. Enigmatic Rob Langer (uncle of future Test star Justin) was next out to the crease.

> I thought, 'Here we go again.' Stumpy out early ... and someone as fast and dangerous as Thommo with the ball in his hand and the breeze at his back. For all our batsmen this prospect was quite unsettling. With the wicket so supportive for pace bowlers ... I remember thinking as I looked at Thommo, 'What's going to happen here?' Grumpy had a 'skull' helmet on under his white washer hat, but there was no such protection for the rest of us ... just pads, gloves and a thin thigh pad.

Two left-handers were now at the crease. Not the easiest task for Thomson, whose slinging action was much more lethal to right-handers because it tended to send the ball in to their body. However, this offered a real opportunity for Thomson's opening partner, left-arm swing bowler Geoff Dymock. Dymock's style meant he'd be able to move the ball away from both batsmen, with the ability to jag one back off the seam on the responsive surface. Which added up to quite a handful.

Dymock's quiet country-lad composure belied the competitive nature that enabled him to take real strides in the game. He bowled mainly at just above medium-pace, with a sharp lift in speed for his yorker and bouncer. His two great attributes were movement through the air *and* control of line and length. This meant, when there was something offering off the wicket—as there certainly was on this WACA Ground pitch—he had an extra invaluable arrow in his quiver. Throughout his career, he played twenty-one Tests (for 78 wickets) and fifteen ODIs (15 wickets).

While the WACA pitch was tailor-made for the bowlers, in such circumstances it's important that quicks don't get too excited and just concentrate on landing the ball in the right areas more often than not. Thomson oozed in and fired them out from that familiar javelin thrower's position, but he was unable to make a further breakthrough. It was the same for Dymock, pushing up into the wind at the other end—luck was in short supply. Charlesworth and Langer were clearly uncomfortable, many times playing and missing, but they were beginning to dig in.

Looking back on that vital partnership for WA, the two men out there were ideally suited. There was the imperturbable nature of Charlesworth—to never allow a near thing to upset his concentration and belief. And there was Langer's ability to play and miss, then hit the next ball out of the park—absolutely untouched by something as 'simple' as being beaten by a good ball! Among his WA teammates Langer was often referred to as 'the streetfighter', after Charles Bronson's role in the movie of the same name. This pugnacious counter-puncher played 44 first-class games for WA, and his 2756 runs came at the excellent average of 43.06. All of which made him good enough to win a WSC contract. Both batsmen tried not to be too perturbed as they watched the ball fly by close to the edge of their bat.

Greg Chappell admitted it took his bowlers a while to get their length right on the fiery pitch, and began to worry about the batsmen getting settled. 'I realised that in the circumstances every run would be critical.'

WA selector Allan Edwards had seen dozens of similar situations on the WACA Ground pitch, especially on the first day of a four-day game when the wicket would play like this. He wasn't feeling too alarmed for his batting side. 'There certainly were a lot of play-and-misses. It wasn't that unusual for Rob Langer to do that—then he'd whack the next ball for four!'

The score was 20 for the loss of Laird's wicket when Chappell decided to remove the fast and furious Thomson—4 overs, 1–10. It was a tough decision for the Queensland captain. On the one hand, Thomson was a trump card, but Chappell had seen the effect of Dymock's medium-pacers—at times almost unplayable at the other end. Plus, Thommo was finding it difficult to get into rhythm. Chappell decided to keep 4 overs from his star quickie up his sleeve and wait and see if the track dried out.

> Thomson: It's been suggested that because of the greasy nature of the wicket I wasn't able to get a good foothold. I'm not sure about that. What I do know is that after the first couple of times on the WACA Ground, whenever I played there I wanted better spikes on my boots.

You'd come from the eastern states, where you wanted worn spikes, to a totally different situation. Before games [in Perth] I would give my boots to Roy Abbott, the groundsman—with a request that he sharpen the spikes for me. He'd take them into the shed and bring them back more like running spikes. There was another thing for me about bowling from the southern end at the ground. It would always take me an hour or so to get used to the run-up. You had to climb up a lot to the pitch area, which then looked as though it was falling away from you when you got there. I found it very hard initially to get on balance, which, of course, is so important for a fast bowler. In the longer form of game you could just get away with it, but in the short form it could be a nightmare. You just didn't have enough time to get settled down. I used to love it when the wind favoured me bowling from the northern end, because the approach there was so much less of a climb.

As it turned out, Queensland's trump card in attack didn't even come back for a second crack at the WA batsmen. On the face of it he had provided a sharp edge for his captain: A wicket and just six scoring strokes out of 32 deliveries. An impressive economy rate of 1.87 from his 4 overs. Chappell had taken a punt on the ability of the slower seamers in his line-up ... and it was a decision that, in the main, paid handsome dividends. However, for Charlesworth and Langer, regardless of Thomson's struggle on the pitch, watching him leave the bowling attack lifted their confidence.

Charlesworth: Our biggest break, after Thommo had struggled with his footing, was the fact that Denis Schuller then came on downwind and he, too, couldn't

DOWN, BUT NOT OUT—Ric Charlesworth manages to get the wayward Denis Schuller away behind square leg.

stand up. We were able to take some easy runs from his bowling.

Langer agrees:

> I recall a sense of immense relief when Greg took Thommo off after 4 overs and brought Schuller on. I couldn't understand at the time, still don't, why he would have taken him off. Schuller couldn't find a good line and length and that got us out of the hole Thommo and Dymock had us in.

Schuller's spell was a mini-disaster for Chappell. The left-armer was a wayward character, if ever there was one in Australian cricket. Long hair, shirt unbuttoned almost down to the waist … often looking more like a renegade from the set of a dark movie than a cricketer—very much his own man. He was an engaging player, but perhaps a little too hot-headed for the situation that day. His bowling was all over the place. He conceded 10 off his first over, and then watched a six go sailing over the backward square leg fence off the first ball of his second over, which cost 12.

Those 22 runs in 2 overs turned out to be significant for WA. Chappell recognised the undisciplined spell as an early turning point in the game.

> We needed to bowl WA out for a gettable total, but when those runs started leaking I thought the game might be getting away from us. Short, wide and full—I think he was too excited.

The memory of those two overs is etched in Denis Schuller's mind.

I think it could have been a little bit to do with the amount of Swan Lager consumed the night before. I should have pulled a hamstring getting out of bed! Seriously, though, I tried to bowl a containing length—it just didn't come off. Plus, I reckon twelve of those runs were French cuts by Ric Charlesworth—who, incidentally, claimed that he hit me for six ... but it was Rob Langer who did that.

Queensland's keeper and vice-captain, John Maclean, looked on in dismay. 'Poor old Schuller got some stick. He tried to bounce the WA bats and Greg was really pissed off that we let Charlesworth and Langer make so many.'

At the other end Dymock was plugging away, having found his line and length—and moving the ball disconcertingly both through the air and off the wicket. Many times the WA pair parried and missed. There was a real mixture of luck, resoluteness and bravado in their partnership, and they managed to stay together for 44 minutes, during which time they scored 42 priceless runs.

> Charlesworth: When we got the score to 50, with only the early loss of Bruce Laird, I was actually thinking it's not too bad out here.

For WA skipper Rod Marsh there was something of a false dawn.

> During that partnership I thought we were progressing pretty well ... and they weren't slow about it, either. The first 50 coming off 11 overs and one ball. Helped, of course, by Schuller's 2 overs! But we were all sitting

back in the dressing room thinking we were on the way to a good total, which we'd then try to defend.

BREAKTHROUGH—Geoff Dymock finds a way through Rob Langer's defences to end the most productive stand in the WA innings.

But just as the home team began to feel confident, the situation, as so often happens in truly great cricket matches, took a sudden turn. Dymock, wheeling down his sixth over on the trot, claimed Langer's wicket. Bowled while playing across the line, looking to hit the ball through the on-side. Langer had made 15. In the context of the WA innings, a score worth many, many more.

For a while there, the expected had become the unexpected. Now the unexpected would become the expected again. Enter Kim Hughes.

A flawed diamond

Kim Hughes

Kim Hughes is the most gifted batsman I have ever seen. Not the best, the most gifted. Okay, the sublime skills and delicate touch of David Gower, Majid Khan, Mark Waugh and Damien Martyn could make the trip to a ground more worthwhile, but Kim Hughes always promised more. On song, he was the mega entertainer. He possessed every shot in the book. The only problem lay in his brain. He wanted to play them all … off every ball! Far too often he would bring about his own downfall through an act of wanton exuberance. That's an important part of the reason why lesser human beings can show a career average in the 50s, while Hughes's 70 Tests produced a figure in the mid-30s. He was like the profligate spender who had little or no concern for the bank balance.

But would you rather watch Allan Border craft one of his twenty-seven Test centuries or allow a Kim Hughes cameo to wrap itself around you? I'd want a Border or a Geoff Boycott batting for my life—he gets out, I die—but there was something almost unique about Kim Hughes. Let me give you one example—the 1980 Centenary Test at Lord's—running down the wicket and going down on one knee to flay the ball like a shot out of a high-powered rifle to the cover point boundary. The England fieldsman a metre off its path shaking his head in wonderment at what had just gone by. Worth treble the price of entry!

Hughes in full flight was something akin to a buccaneer, swishing his cutlass at anything within reach. For him, there was no risk not worth taking. That's why we all adored him, crazy risks and all.

Dennis Lillee and Kim Hughes had lots in common, and there was an amazing sense of anticipation and promise surrounding them both. At the start of both their careers, if you were in the Perth cricket 'scene', you knew they were coming long before they arrived. Word was out about a young tearaway quick and, not long after, this flashy young batsman. You hadn't seen them, but you already 'knew' them. The same sense of anticipation came some time later, this time with another batsman of great promise—Damien Martyn.

Like most who make it high up the ladder in the game, cricket coursed thickly through Hughes's veins when he was a young lad. His potential first emerged with the juniors in the WA country town of Geraldton, where he made the junior country week team as an eleven-year-old. He made progress, which accelerated in leaps and bounds when the family moved to Perth, and at fourteen he came under the spell of a crusty little campaigner called Frank Parry. Parry had played some first-grade cricket in Perth and, while you sensed he knew a bit about batting, you later found out that he knew a lot more about hot-gospelling. He constantly blew drafts of warm wind into his young prodigy's ears. He threw (perhaps a better word would be 'lobbed') countless thousands of balls at him in the nets and rained praise on the youngster when, inevitably, he made a half volley or a full toss of them and thrashed them away—feeding the young man's innate cavalier nature.

One evening, after Hughes had made a duck in a club game, Parry was on the phone at the family home—asking to speak to his despondent protégé. 'Listen, Champ, I've seen Bradman and Harvey and all the great players … that was the best-made duck I've ever seen.' Hughes replied, 'Frankie, was it as good as that?' 'Champ, there's only you and Bradman. The rest can't bat.'

The brashness that inevitably evolved from Parry's incessant chants would be part of what took Hughes to the brink of greatness. Most of what came out of Parry's mouth was good advice, albeit at times a bit over the top. Mostly it was helpful, though I'm not so sure that it always pointed Hughes in the right direction. 'Champ,' Parry told him one day, 'you'll not only play for Australia, you'll also captain Australia!' Right, on both counts. But would Hughes live to regret his subsequent fervent pursuit of the captaincy? If he didn't, certainly I wasn't alone in wishing he'd been satisfied with just being one of the best and most exciting bladesmen. Ever.

Hughes made his senior club debut for Subiaco at the age of fifteen. The pump was primed. But the flow was hesitant. He made a brave 40 against Lillee in a club game—and a maiden club century against the very strong Midland-Guildford attack.

As a sixteen-year-old he was added to the WA senior squad, but after three average seasons in club cricket he was glossed over. Recognising the potential—and pestered by a zealous band of Hughes followers—the WA selectors recalled him and in November 1974 named him as twelfth man. After carrying the drinks for three games in a row, impatience took a hold on Hughes and he left for Adelaide, determined to break into the struggling SA team. Nothing happened. Four months later he was back in WA. Look at me now, chaps! The selectors did. They picked him for Western Australia's opening game of the 1975–76 Sheffield Shield season against New South Wales, and on 2 November Kimberley John Hughes stepped out onto the WACA Ground on a long and mercurial journey. I played in that game, and to say that a skyrocket was launched would be an understatement. It was more like a space probe leaving Cape Canaveral.

Facing a near-Test attack, including Lennie Pascoe, Gary Gilmour, David Colley and Kerry O'Keeffe, he plundered runs to all parts of the ground. Displaying the balance and poise of a ballet dancer, and the confidence of a five-year veteran, he moved down the wicket and mauled the bowling, pace and spin alike. Bringing out a shot that would become his pièce de résistance—the cover drive from a position with his right knee on the ground. It was truly heady stuff. He became the fifth West Australian to score a century on debut and was finally dismissed, caught on the long-on boundary (with the fieldsman's bottom resting on the pickets) for an unforgettable 119. He was out in the final over before tea and, had the catch cleared the fence, he would have posted a century in the session. It was 'Champ' alright. Hughes added 60 more in the second innings and we all wondered just how many more glorious centuries we would witness that season.

But the pump had run out of water. In twelve remaining innings of the Shield season he passed 50 only once (though he did make a second-innings century against the touring West Indians). A bright light had been doused. We senior Western Australian players watched one opportunity after another being frittered away, largely through acts of gross impetuosity. He just didn't get the 'rhythm' of batting—of understanding the dimensions that went to building an innings. Of the words 'patience' and 'shot selection'—picking the right ball to go after.

This was something that plagued us through the winter months that followed. So much so that when the new season opened with a four-game tour of the eastern states we boarded the plane for Adelaide with a plan—for Kim. As one of the three tour selectors, I joined captain Rod Marsh, his deputy Dennis Lillee and team coordinator Daryl Foster in a special meeting with the young gun. Mission: Teach him the fundaments of building an innings, make him understand that it was more important to make lots of hundreds at a reasonable lick than to go out there with a view to smashing the bowling and making only the odd stunning century.

At the conclusion of a pre-game team meeting at our motel, we sat Kim down on a chair in the middle of the room and formed a semicircle around him. Rod led the attack. He underlined our thinking on the mission, stating that it would be best for Kim to set targets when he went to the crease: 'To bat for drinks ... bat for lunch ... bat for drinks ... bat for tea ...' And so on, finishing with the suggestion that it would be just fine to set yourself the target of making your century in 240 minutes (which was a bit of a benchmark in those days).

We all fortified Rod's words. Through all of this Kim was nodding, to the point I was convinced he was taking it in. Rod then went to the closer, ending with, 'Right Kim … you've been in for 240 minutes … how many are you?' At which the subject of our interest looked thoughtfully towards the ceiling, then said with a toothy grin, 'Eight hundred!' That was the Kim Hughes of those days. Impish, mischievous and adorable. Particularly loved by Marsh and Lillee, who, might I say, were imbued with a similar Aussie larrikin spirit.

At the end of that game in Adelaide, when Kim top-scored in the first innings and WA won, Dennis requested that a bottle of Bacardi be brought to the rooms. It was the old bull and the young bull. After a couple of mixes Dennis announced he'd be drinking it straight—from the bottle. Kim's bombast at its height, he said he would, too. Only trouble was, Lillee only made bubbles and drank very little, while his drinking mate took great swigs and was soon talking another language.

One of the reasons for the flush of success WA teams enjoyed in that period was the involvement of the wives and girlfriends. One time we all went away to a resort for a weekend. Late one night we were sitting around playing the inevitable drinking game. Kim kept being caught and, trying to slow things down, started complaining about the rules. To which one of the older wives said, 'Get on with it Kim, we were playing this game when you were still in nappies.' Whereupon he rose on unsteady feet, placed hands on hips, leant forward and said, 'Oh alright, Dame Nellie Melba!'

It wasn't all fun, but when Hughes was around Marsh and Lillee in those days there were heaps of laughs. How that was to change. And it all began to shift not that long after that game in Adelaide—revolving around the recruitment of Australian players for the breakaway World Series Cricket competition. It was a case of was he, or was he not? ... approached to sign up. The WSC side says to this day, 'No.' Hughes still says, 'Yes.' And at that fraught and fractured time in Australian cricket, he went further to say he hadn't accepted the offer because 'he didn't care to'.

This was like a red rag to a bull for the players at the sharp end of the WSC troupe—in particular Ian Chappell, Marsh and Lillee. And it would haunt Hughes for the remainder of his Test career, and, finally, cause him to resign the Australian captaincy, which he had so coveted. Hughes was with the Australian team for the ill-fated tour of England in 1977, which was played under the cloud of WSC. He was chosen to make his debut in the Fifth Test at The Oval and would have made no friends when he publicly claimed he'd only been picked as a scapegoat for the team's lack of success. In his only innings he took 34 balls to score a single to get off the mark ... and that was it.

The absence of Australia's best during the WSC years meant chances of Test selection were greater for Hughes the batsman. However, too often a rush of blood cost him his wicket—like going after Ian Botham on the first ball of a spell in Melbourne and holing out, and charging Bob Willis the first ball after lunch, to be caught at cover. Much of it was painful to watch from the commentator's seat. It seemed as though he would never learn, or that he didn't want to change his ways. Then, in March, 1979, like a dream come true for him, he tumbled into the captaincy. Graham Yallop had to withdraw from the Second Test against Pakistan and, in front of his home crowd, Hughes became the first West Australian to captain his country. Joy and pride abounded in the Hughes camp, but the drums had begun beating away in the distance and, when WSC and the Australian Cricket Board agreed to a reunification, the matter of captaincy beyond that day bubbled to the surface.

Ian Chappell had led WSC Australia, but had no desire to continue his career. Brother Greg had been captain before the big schism. There was also Rod Marsh, who'd displayed great leadership qualities as captain of WA for the two seasons leading up to WSC. And then there was Kim Hughes, captain during the WSC years. Existing wounds gaped open when Greg Chappell got the nod with Hughes as his deputy. Marsh overlooked! Lillee miffed! Ian Chappell, now a television broadcaster, also offside, because in his opinion Hughes was a distant third in any three-way contest for the post with his brother and Marsh.

So began a horrible period in the life of Hughes and the Australian team. Ian Chappell constantly niggling from the sidelines, Marsh refusing to serve as Hughes's deputy when Greg Chappell declined to go on tours and Hughes was elevated, and Hughes and Lillee clearly standing apart. Twice the Australian Cricket Board voted on the matter—and both times a narrow margin went Hughes's way. The 'Cold War' continued. Lillee consistently bowled bouncers at Hughes in the nets, saying it was only to toughen him up, while Hughes remained tight-lipped publicly on the practice. Plus, there was open on-field argument over field placings.

Meanwhile, the punctuation of the Centenary Test at Lord's in 1980. I was part of the commentary team for the ABC television coverage and witnessed at first hand a true Kim Hughes tour de force. He was playing on the main stage, the home of cricket in a game full of historical significance, attended by most of those still living who had ever played in an Ashes Test. Hughes rose to the occasion, and played up to the audience in the finest possible manner.

Rain curtailed play on the first three days. Coincidentally, this meant Hughes was on stage for all of those days, compiling an exquisite 117. He was at his flamboyant best—at one moment dancing down the wicket to flay the ball down the ground, and at another rising to full height to dispatch short-pitched deliveries with equal disdain. Fourteen fours and three sixes. If that wasn't enough to have hardened old campaigners (those who weren't in the tent at the back of the Pavilion deep in reminiscence) nodding their heads in approval, there was more to come. And it was even better. The England first innings closed and the blond dasher found himself back centre stage late on the fourth day. Because of the time lost, the game was gone. It was time for some fun.

Two strokes in that cavalier knock of 84 stand out like pulsating beacons in my memory. The first—batting at the Pavilion End to an Ian Botham who looked about as jaded as the fourth-day pitch. Three men patrolled the cover boundary in front of the Mound Stand, one just behind point, around to the third at cover. A challenge. Hughes departed the crease before the ball had left the bowler's hand and when he met it, on the half volley, he was on his right knee, his bat scything down on the ball. I swear it scorched over the ropes before any of those three men had even moved. The second—on guard at the Nursery End to an equally pedestrian Chris Old. Clearing the fence at Lord's in this game so far had been mere bagatelle, but now the rampaging Hughes set out to go one better. He almost ran down the wicket to meet the ball just on the rise … and sent it sailing and soaring on to the top deck of the Pavilion. Old hands had never seen such an outcome (though some muttered about the legend of Gilbert Jessop). Others just shook their heads in disbelief.

The fact that the Test was drawn was of little matter. Those who had five-day tickets had seen some of the most beautiful, breathtaking batting imaginable. Hughes, who had batted on all five days of the game, scored a total of 201 runs, including twenty-five fours and five sixes—the only cricketer to have hit a six on all five days of a Test. Not surprisingly, he was named Man-of-the-Match.

For Kim Hughes, his most personal batting achievement, fulfilling his sense of prophecy and incredible self-belief, was a Test played in Adelaide over the Australia Day long weekend in 1981. It was Hughes's twenty-seventh birthday. The opponent was India, and the wicket offered a bit to their men of spin—Dilip Doshi and Shivlal Yadav. Hughes had always maintained that spin of any class was akin to a gift from the heavens, but he was coming off a very lean run and the wolves were barking, if not howling, before the game—suggesting that he needed a score here to shore up his position in the side. His reaction to these murmurs was to boast to his family that he would make a century for each of his twin sons, Simon and Sean, born a fortnight earlier. The resultant innings was a fine blend of caution and aggression—in the best Hughes style. Racing down the wicket to the spinners, and standing to full height to crack the quicks back down the ground. The century mark passed with a classical cover drive from the down-on-one-knee position. The double coming with support from Australia's number eleven, Lennie Pascoe. Hughes was on 193 when Pascoe arrived, but he reached the magical figure with a hammering drive to remember, off Yadav. The masterpiece ended on 213, and later that day the father made it clear: a century each for his new twin boys!

I was also fortunate to have been in the commentator's chair at another Kim Hughes gem. At the MCG on Boxing Day of the same year, Australia were playing against the West Indies. Batting first, Australia were 4–26 when Hughes was joined by Dirk Wellham. Hughes was on 70 (and the Australian total 155) when Terry Alderman came in at number eleven. Against all odds Hughes went to reach 100, out of 198. It was an absolutely extraordinary innings, in the face of Holding, Roberts, Garner and Croft on a dicey track. Hughes threw his bat at everything the Windies quicks could muster, and won the day. His team went on to win the match and the plaudits flew in. Andy Roberts: 'He took up the challenge and it paid off for him. It was a great innings.' The *Wisden 100* (a ranking of the Top 100 Test Innings of all time), placed that knock at number nine. It ranks even higher for me. Perhaps number one! This time Hughes dedicated the innings to his ailing father-in-law, Rix Davidson, who died a few weeks later.

The on-again, off-again captaincy situation did Hughes no favours. Neither did the running fire of series against the mighty West Indians. As he struggled both as a captain and with the bat, friends counselled him to forgo the leadership and concentrate on his batting skills. He would have none of it, deflecting the knives and soldiering on. And so the pressure mounted. I could see it coming to a head during the First Test of the 1984–85 series against the West Indies at the Gabba. You could tell that the usual Kim Hughes strut, shoulders back and head thrust forward, was absent. Late on the final day, 26 November 1984, I watched off-air from the ABC broadcast position at the southern end of the ground as Hughes and team manager Bob Merriman appeared to be in and out of meetings. I said to fellow commentator Drew Morphett, 'We need to go to the post-match press conference. I reckon something's going to happen.'

And it did. Hughes walked in holding a piece of paper. At the conclusion of the usual questions about the game, he said, 'Gentlemen, before you go I have something to read.' He looked a broken man. Part of the way through his announcement that he was resigning the captaincy, with tears streaming down his face, he could go no further. He handed the piece of paper to Merriman and said 'you read it', then walked out of the room. It was a very sad moment indeed. But somehow I felt relieved for him. A huge weight had been lifted from his shoulders.

Now, I thought, for some more vintage Kim Hughes, free from the captaincy. But, even sadder, we witnessed this marvellous talent limp out of the game. His final seven innings for Australia (Tests and one-dayers) produced a meagre 7 runs from 38 balls faced. Then he chose to captain Australia in the rebel tours to South Africa, played a little more for WA, and finished his career with Natal, where he suffered the indignity of being dropped to the second team. Before scoring 4 and 9 in his final first-class game.

In the final analysis, most will agree that Kim Hughes possessed stellar talents with the bat in hand, but there was flaw in this rare diamond ... and for me it revolved around his desire to captain the Australian team. His record of four wins and thirteen losses from twenty-eight games at the helm tells a story of hard times, and I like to believe that, without the burdens of leadership—and at liberty to just bat beautifully and majestically in his own inimitable fashion—Kim Hughes would have ended his career as one of the very best. With broad smiles, rather than tears, on his sunny face.

The floodgates open

As far as WA cricket followers were concerned, Kim Hughes was the prodigal son. He was twenty-one when he made a century on debut for the state at this very ground, setting the place alight with a flamboyant display of stroke-making. Just over a year later his flame was still burning brightly, though he'd had a rather ordinary start to the season—just three half-centuries in four Shield games and another half-century in WA's Gillette Cup qualifying game. Still, with WA reasonably placed on 50, for the loss of Laird and Langer, there was an understandable purpose in the young man's stride as he went to the crease.

If anything, at this stage WA was winning the battle. You just knew that this was going be a difficult batting wicket all day. And, for now, on paper there was still plenty of batting to come. Charlesworth was well set and, in Hughes, WA had a player quite capable of taking the bowling—any sort of bowling, in any conditions—by the scruff of the neck and giving it a good shake. There were plenty of overs remaining and at that moment there was no real sense of concern in the home team dressing room. But there soon would be!

Hughes survived the remaining ball of what was Dymock's sixth over—but only just. The ball nipped back in from off and struck him a painful blow on the inside of his right thigh. After a couple of vigorous rubs, he walked down for a mid-pitch chat with Charlesworth, keen for the cut and thrust to continue after Langer's departure.

Meanwhile, Greg Chappell had no option but to take Denis Schuller out of the attack. Especially with a hungry Kim Hughes now out in the middle. For the Queensland skipper there was far too much risk of a further serious leakage of runs. He turned, instead, to medium-pacer Phil Carlson—not a front-line bowler, but very handy *and* guaranteed to extract whatever there was to be taken from the conditions.

Carlson was a quiet achiever. A sound middle-order batsman and a canny bowler, with prodigious movement of the ball through the air in the right conditions and a fine sense of control of line and length. He holds the distinction of scoring a century and taking a total of 10 wickets in a first-class game for Queensland. And played two Tests and two ODIs for Australia, during the WSC years.

The change immediately paid off for a relieved Chappell. Trapping the stubborn Charlesworth leg before with his very first delivery. Bill Lawry supported the decision. 'A refreshing change, to see an umpire not frightened to give a batsman out.' It was a wonderful follow-up breakthrough for Queensland. Two wickets had fallen in the space of three balls. Charlesworth had faced 55 deliveries in his stay of 66 minutes for 25 runs. In terms of the contest, solid gold stuff for the home side. WA now 3–50, but still seemingly not beyond building a defendable total.

The elegant Craig Serjeant strode purposefully out to join Hughes. A tall right-hander who was a prolific scorer on the on-side, Serjeant would enjoy a meteoric rise to international recognition. Less than a year after his debut for WA, he was chosen for the 1977 tour to England and played in the Lord's Test—making 81 on debut. However, aside from a century against the West Indies at Guyana in 1978, his career figures from twelve Tests and three ODIs didn't measure up to the potential he had shown. And this Gillette Cup semifinal, certainly, would not turn out to be a batting highlight in his career.

What was to follow on the WACA Ground was a storm of devastating proportions for the home side. The new bowling duo of Dymock and Carlson proved to be absolute wreckers in this phase of the game—the floodgates were opened. Conditions were near perfect for men of swing and seam. The nature of the pitch surface meant the ball suffered little scarring from contact. It was a batsman's nightmare—big movement through the air, followed too often with deviation off the wicket when the ball landed on the proud seam. Says Charlesworth, 'They [the medium-pacers] could stand up without any difficulty. And they moved it quite violently.'

Dymock seized the moment and, following Carlson's first-ball success, completely dominated the batsmen, taking wickets in his sixth and seventh overs. First he added new batsman Serjeant (leg before without offering a stroke to a ball that jagged back from the off).

> Serjeant: It was the first time I'd seen Geoff Dymock at
> close quarters and the first three balls were pitching
> on middle and seaming away to off. My inexperience
> then showed, because he also had the in-swinger to the

right-hander, which he produced with the next ball. Again, I didn't offer a shot and was out plumb leg before.

WA now 4–51.

Then Marsh, usually a strong, even dominant, player in such circumstances, arrived to take up the cudgels. He came and went first ball … spooning a Dymock half-volley to Viv Richards at square leg. Bill Lawry summed it up. 'He made the cardinal sin of playing across the line of the ball.'

Then, to cap off a match-turning spell for Queensland, Carlson chimed in to bowl Hughes with a brute of a swinging delivery. The young prodigy had watched as three of his team-mates had fallen foul of a ball that was still as shiny as a new cherry and, with a seam virtually untouched, playing all sorts of tricks. He had been there for 18 minutes and faced 6 balls. Hughes—who normally relished such a challenge and would meet it head-on—couldn't handle the stinging conditions at his home ground that day.

WA 6–51. The cream of the middle order—Kim Hughes, Craig Serjeant and Rod Marsh—all gone without scoring a run. In the space of 15 minutes and twenty-one balls, 5 wickets had fallen for just one run—a leg bye. As Serjeant and Hughes, in particular, had found, the movement had an element of a mesmeric effect. Almost unbelievable.

> Hughes: It was almost the slower you bowled the more it did and, against our initial fears, it was the medium-pacers who turned out to be a real handful.

Though still quite young and inexperienced, the perennially ebullient Hughes was something of a beacon for WA's batting performance—such a positive influence. His departure for a duck, on top of the others to depart in a hurry, was in danger of totally derailing the WA innings.

For Rob Langer it was numbing to watch. And stunning.

> When I was dismissed I was sitting at the back of the dressing room, slowly taking off my gear and remaining there for a little while, thinking about the battle it had been out there. All of a sudden there was this Hay Street of players, coming and going—first Grumpy came in, then Sarge, Bacchus and Clag. Mayhem!

Serjeant was stunned, too.

> When your team's batting and you're in the dressing room, you look for signs as to what's going on out in the middle. The first thing I noticed was how many times our batsmen were playing and missing. I thought to myself, 'It must be doing a lot out there … the guys aren't laying a bat on this.' When we saw Rob Langer play and miss it was nothing unusual, because he would always play through the line so that if the ball moved more than a little he would miss it. He was actually more technically suited to this type of wicket than most of the rest of us. But Ric was actually sparring at them and going much closer to getting an edge. You thought, it must be doing a bit, because he was a good leaver of the ball.

Greg Chappell, even in his wildest dreams, could not have imagined the carnage that he had just unleashed on the WACA Ground. His team were now well and truly in the driver's seat … needing only a quick tidy-up, then some sensible batting. The Gillette Cup final, for the second year in a row, was tantalisingly close at hand.

Quick-change act

Bruce Yardley

Two cricketers I played with for WA enjoyed a successful Test career after 'reinventing' their game. I deeply admire them both for deciding that enough wasn't good enough and for being prepared to do something about it.

The first was Ross Edwards. Son of a former WA wicketkeeper, Edwards first played for the state in 1964 as a 'keeper–batsman. But he was thwarted in this pursuit, first by the presence in the squad of Gordon Becker, then by the arrival of a young and very promising Rod Marsh. Realising he was forever heading up a blind alley, Edwards finally put away the 'keeping gear and set out with a purpose—to make himself a better batsman, and first and foremost to cement a place in the WA side in that role. In the half-dark, when most were packing up to go home, he'd beg somebody (often me) to throw balls at him while he batted with only a stump in hand. At the same time he knew he must develop skills as a fieldsman—and to grow a fieldsman's throwing arm. (He ended up doing this with such success that at the peak of his game he was considered one of the best covers men in the world.)

True to his promise, Edwards not only played for WA as a batsman, making four centuries and topping the averages for WA in the 1971–72 season, but he also played for Australia, heading to England for the 1972 Ashes series and making a century in his second Test match. The end product of this remarkable renaissance was that he retired after a twenty-Test career with 1171 runs and a solid average of 40.37. Hats off.

The second reinvention cricketer was Bruce Yardley, or 'Roo', who came into the WA side against Queensland at the WACA Ground in December 1966. Believe it or not, he was our down-wind new-ball bowler—and opened the attack with myself. (Surely one of the least lethal opening attacks ever assembled in a Sheffield Shield game!) He sent down a total of 19 overs and took one wicket for 57 runs.

One little scenario from that day rests deep in my memory—Yardley sending down a bouncer to incoming batsman Peter Burge, one of the great hookers of the day. The ball disappeared over the fence at forward square leg. To our utter amazement, another, similarly innocuous, half-tracker followed. It went the same way as its predecessor. Only further. We later asked Yardley what that was all about. Turns out our captain, Murray Vernon, who was standing at mid-off, had told him Burge was susceptible to a short one early in his innings. Then, after the first one disappeared, had said, 'Give him another one …'

Being of slight build and medium height, Yardley was never going to be a great fast bowler—and at the time his future appeared to be seriously limited. After that one game, he was dropped and didn't play for WA again until he made one appearance in the 1970–71 season. Again he headed off to club-land.

Along the way, though, he had developed a well-disguised slower ball, delivered from his pace bowler's run-up. This was basically an off-spin delivery. A club-mate saw a different future for Yardley—and suggested he convert to bowling only that style of ball. In other words, become a spinner. He made the change, slowly but successfully, and returned to the WA side as a spinner in the 1973–74 season. By January 1978, he was trying on the baggy green cap. At the age of 30. Job done!

I have often wondered what it would have been like trying to survive and score off England's Derek Underwood's deadly accuracy as a spinner at slow medium pace. On a wicket offering a bit of assistance, there was no hope of getting down the wicket to make a half-volley. Same with Yardley. Only he was able to make the ball loop and drop into the wind, and then break back the other way, with loads of bounce. He had been a baseball pitcher and took an unusual grip—spreading the middle and ring fingers, rather than the index and middle—and imparted great overspin to wonderful effect. He went on to play 33 Tests and take 126 wickets at the good average of 31.63. And it should have been more. There was absolutely no accounting for the decision not to include him in the touring party for England in 1981. He could have been the difference between the two sides in a series that England won against the odds. Returning to the side for the following Australian summer, he took 38 wickets in Tests against the West Indies and Pakistan and was voted International Cricketer-of-the-Year. However, equally unbelievably, again he was overlooked, this time for the World Cup in England. Not long after, he called it quits.

Apart from being one of the most likable guys you'd ever meet, Yardley was a real livewire in the dressing room and on the field. A great team man who could dance the pants off John Travolta. His effervescence and exuberance were infectious. Never a dull moment. Great hands in the gully and a splendid outfielder. And, yes, there was more. Yardley the batsman! His stance was a classic: Legs set wide apart, resulting in a real crouch as he waited for the bowler to come at him. Grip low on the handle. He batted down the order where his scything blows against the quicks—often played from a position a little out towards square leg—could be quite devastating. At the SCG in November 1976 I was almost an innocent bystander in a stand worth 132 … while Yardley carved up the attack, to be on 97 when stumps were drawn to end the game. Scintillating stuff! Plus, those who saw it still talk about his 74 against a full-strength West Indies attack in the Second Test at Barbados in 1978. They threw everything but the kitchen sink at Yardley—and he threw it all back at them! Jeff Thomson batted with him that day:

> When I was on strike I was getting half-volleys, but when Roo was on strike it was completely different. He was running around and flaying away at them. Then Joel [Garner] bowled him this great yorker and Roo was away with a bit of room and thrashed it through the covers. I was pissing myself.

The sun was setting for Yardley when he took part in Australia's first tour of Sri Lanka in 1983. He took 7 wickets, including a five-wicket haul, in what proved to be his final Test. But he never forgot the island nation. In 1997, he took over as their national coach. During that time he got to know record-breaking spinner Muttiah Muralitharan and had an influence over his career, encouraging him to develop the (other-way) doosra, and was a stout defender of the legality of the spinner's action. Also during that time he faced up to a personal tragedy. Yardley was in the West Indies on tour with Sri Lanka when he lost sight in his left eye. He returned to Perth, where the problem was diagnosed as a melanoma and the eye was removed. After finishing with Sri Lanka, Yardley took up the post as coach of the Singapore Cricket Association. His most recent coaching role was with the WA Indigenous squad in 2010—and he guided them to victory in the national Imparja Cup tournament.

Yardley's love affair with all things Sri Lanka lives on. When the 2004 tsunami devastated the island he flew in, armed with $10,000 worth of donated medical supplies and some work clothes. Much was achieved in a month. It was there that he met a young local lass called Chaturika. Empathising with the fact her left eye was missing, he made arrangements for her to be flown to Perth, where a prosthesis similar to his own was fitted. She has since married. And her smile is as wide and beautiful as that of the man we all call 'Roo'. Always active … always positive … always looking forward.

A false dawn

You might well ask the question—one that would surely have been buzzing around the WACA Ground as Bruce Yardley strode out to join the author: How does a batting team recover from such a disastrous collapse? It bears repeating. Five wickets gone in 15 devastating minutes for the addition of just one run. And that a leg bye. The Queenslanders were understandably cock-a-hoop. Keep the ball rolling. At this rate, look at a run chase of, say, 60. Goodbye WA ... hello Queensland!

In limited-overs cricket in those days you could never quite be sure how many runs by the first team batting could constitute a winning score. But as Yardley and I met in the middle of the pitch and exchanged pleasantries, we both knew that 51 was way short of enough. From the relative comfort of the dressing room I had seen the pride of our middle order crumble. Then I'd seen Carlson sneak a gem through Kim Hughes's defences to rattle the timbers. What next, I wondered.

Of all the blokes you've been to 'war' with over the years, perhaps there was none better than Bruce Yardley for such a situation. Ice-cold temperament, unflappable—and quite unorthodox. From the sanctuary of the non-striker's end, I watched Roo ask the umpire for his guard. Loudly and confidently. Then take a cursory glance around the field and collapse into that unforgettable Yardley crouch. Waiting for Phil Carlson to send down another hand grenade. My thought was, 'Roo's a good chance to have some fun here.' And Roo did just that. He sliced into the Queensland medium-pacers in one of his typical cameo stays at the crease. Okay, he had a bit of look at things before taking a single off Carlson but with only 15 of 40 overs gone, there was plenty of time. With Roo, literally anything could happen. Then he sized up Geoff Dymock's left-armers at the other end and simply glided one behind point for a boundary. Roo would often just throw his bat at it, but in this stroke there was some exquisite timing. The first positive for WA in some time drew a droll comment from Richie Benaud: 'A welcome sight for WA supporters at the ground.'

Four balls later and Dymock had finished his excellent spell. Eight overs, 3–20.

Benaud again:

> There is the end of a fine spell of bowling—in any class
> of cricket—but in a limited-overs fixture such as this is
> it has been an immaculate performance.

It seemed a relief to see the back of Dymock, but it wasn't going to get any easier for WA from that end. The following over from Carlson was a bountiful one for WA—Yardley lofted him through the covers for four and picked up a couple of twos. But then Greg Chappell took over at the northern end, and his first over was a promising one. Chappell's slower pace and high release would also prove to be a handful.

> Dennis Lillee: I remember watching as we batted and the ball was swinging and moving sharply off the deck when it landed on the seam. Phil Carlson and Greg Chappell were just about unplayable. All their bowlers beat the bat time after time. It had been a respectable position [at 2–50], but then, all of a sudden, everybody started getting out. I thought that the wicket must have been drying out.

While his partner (me) sat on the splice, Yardley pushed on in inimitable fashion. Playing a classical front-foot square drive off Carlson that scorched its way to the boundary. It was a moment to give the forlorn WA fans something to cheer about. Shot of the day, in fact. Then … anything but the shot of the day. Yardley had a wild slog at Carlson and the ball floated high in the breeze towards Thomson at mid-on. The Queenslander barely got hands on the ball and there was relief in the WA camp as it tumbled to the ground. Richie Benaud summed it up. 'He may have been allowing for the breeze … but I'm not too sure Thommo will allow for things like that when a catch goes up.'

But then Yardley's luck ran out. Working with a ball that was still almost brand new, Chappell got him—chasing a big, looping out-swinger that was taken cleanly by a diving Maclean. Roo had been the lead player in what turned out to be a vital seventh-wicket stand of 25 for WA. In the context of the innings, his 19 runs were significant.

> Maclean: As the wickets tumbled the feeling in our group was one of high confidence. Even when Yardley

was on the run, we knew WA weren't going to make many. But he and Brayshaw did take it from 6–51 to 76. They should have been joint Man-of-the-Match! Without that stand we would have had a truly manageable chase.

Yardley's departure heralded a second calamitous collapse by WA. Next in was Dennis Lillee, a useful and brave tailender, but less than adequately equipped to be holding out much hope for the home side in these conditions. As often was the case with his batting, he decided that aggression was the way forward. He saw two balls from Chappell go by before one came in the slot and his attempt to clear the man at mid-on fell short.

WA 8–76.

HE'S OUT!—John Maclean completes a fine diving catch to dismiss Bruce Yardley, off the bowling of Greg Chappell.

Craig Serjeant: Towards the end of our innings I looked up at the board and saw all these noughts next to our batsmen's names and I thought, this is simply embarrassing. This was a semifinal, there was a good crowd in the ground and WA cricket was going pretty well at the time ... the game was going to be as good as over in the first couple of hours. It was just lamentable.

When Mick Malone reached the middle it hit me that, in the prevailing conditions, hopes of another rear-guard action were minimal. Mick was a great competitor, as was our number eleven, Wayne Clark, but neither was anything to write home about with bat in hand. If WA was to substantially add to the pathetic total I would have to step up. And hog the strike! Every run added might be worth 10 in another set of circumstances. After taking a single off Carlson—and leaving Malone to survive 3 deliveries—I faced up to a new over from Chappell.

It must have looked like the cardinal mistake—especially in conditions favouring the bowlers—of gifting my wicket in a run-out. But in all honesty I was trying to claim the strike and protect the tailenders. There was very nearly a run in it, too. The ball was played in the forward square leg region ... trouble was, the fielder, Geoff Dymock, being a left-hander, was able to pick up and throw without having to change his angles. The throw beat me by centimetres. As I headed off I couldn't help feeling frustrated: Out there for 37 minutes, 28 deliveries and just 5 runs.

WA 9–77.

Then Wayne Clark, with another nought on the board next to his name, was caught by Thomson at mid-on, off Carlson. It was all over. There was a deathly hush over the WACA Ground as the players left the field. Dismissed for a meagre 77, WA's hopes of advancing to the final were all but shattered. Only three players reaching double figures, with Charlesworth top scorer on 25 … while six hadn't even managed to put a run on the board. It was unthinkable that a team as strong as WA was at that time would have crumbled so meekly. The recriminations abounded in the home team dressing room. It was a complete disaster. Losing their final 4 wickets in the space of sixteen balls. For one run!

Captain Marsh was far from impressed. 'There was a big crowd there and we were all out in dead-on two hours.' Bruce Laird: 'When we collapsed so badly, I couldn't help feeling embarrassed—thinking, "This is disgraceful."'

Disgraceful it was, indeed. WA had managed to survive only 22.5 (eight-ball) overs. No matter how favourable conditions were for the fielding side, this effort had been tantamount to handing victory to the opposition on a plate.

As a playing group, Queensland were over the moon … but their captain knew better.

> Chappell: I thought on that pitch and with our attack and bowling first we would probably dismiss them for an attainable total, but 77 was beyond my wildest expectations. However, I knew that 77 would be no easy chase. I knew Dennis Lillee well enough to know that he would be right in our faces. As I sat down in the dressing room I recognised that Viv and I would need to make the bulk of the runs if we were to win.

Greg Chappell had played enough games in Perth to acknowledge, while he contemplated the task ahead, the fact that it was likely the pitch would have dried out a little and quickened up by the time the run chase got under way.

No appetite

At any sporting venue there are at least two dressing rooms—with one for the home team and one for the visitors. At the WACA Ground on that day in December 1976 the doors to the two rooms were right next to each other, with only a single brick wall separating the teams. As two down-cast and bemused WA batsmen closed one door behind them, eleven very buoyant Queensland fieldsmen walked in and shut their door. While their captain was more circumspect, 'I knew we had a job on our hands', the Queensland team were, understandably, feeling very confident as they contemplated a miniscule run chase.

> Jeff Thomson: There was a warm air of confidence that we could get the runs. There was nobody, outwardly at least, saying we were going to struggle to get them.

In fact, the feeling was that we'd probably get them a couple down.

John Maclean: We really felt we could get to 78 and win it. What happened, I think, was that having Greg and Viv in the team the rest of us were thinking, in the subconscious, that the chase was going to be a cakewalk.

Phil Carlson: There was a confident mood, even a bit blasé, that with our batting line-up we'd get the runs. We knew we'd have a bit of a battle, because any team with Dennis Lillee in it was going to make it a bit hard, but we'd get there alright.

The atmosphere in the WA room, not surprisingly, couldn't have been more different.

Captain Rod Marsh: From the time Greg Chappell called 'tails' and put us in I knew we would struggle. When we were out for such a paltry score I was sure we couldn't win. The rowdy crowd made it feel a bit like a football grand final—and the only way we were going to win at half-time was if we were to kick with the wind in the last *two* quarters!

Meanwhile, his players mulled around in a shell-shocked state, some loudly voicing their disgust and embarrassment. Veteran selector Allan Edwards experienced the mood:

It was a habit [of fellow selector Lawrie Sawle and me] to always go into the dressing room at the end of a day's play—just a brief visit, good day or bad day. Well at the end of the WA innings I went to the room. But I only lasted about ten seconds, because everyone was so wild at what had happened. There was screaming and shouting, and it was no place for an outsider. Particularly Dennis was very upset.

Nobody in the WA camp was keen to walk next door into the lunchroom.

Dennis Lillee: In the break, early as it was because we were out so quickly, I recall being so pissed off with our performance that I threw my lunchtime eating rules out the window. In those days the menu would be either fish and chips or an old piece of leather loosely disguised as steak. Instead of my normal peaches and ice-cream and Sustagen before bowling, I whaled into the fish and chips—thinking it wouldn't make much difference what I ate that day.

Because the WA innings had barely scraped past the halfway mark in their set of 40 overs, it was initially thought there would be a very long luncheon adjournment. At one stage during that break, with victory seemingly just around the corner for Queensland, an idea was floated by a grim WACA management for a second game between the two sides to give the spectators some value for their entry money. A shortened short-form game was proposed—which could have been a forerunner for the T20 style of game that would sweep in with a rush a quarter of a century later.

Mick Malone, meanwhile, was making his own plans for the expected empty afternoon. 'I do remember during the lunch break a couple of us talking about trying to organise a barbecue with our wives and girlfriends for that afternoon.'

Thirty minutes later, though, any thoughts for what to do after the game were put on hold. The umpires knocked on the dressing room doors to call the players out. It was 'game on' again.

A grim-faced WA captain gathered his players around at the dressing room door, to lead them out to defend the indefensible.

> Rod Marsh: With only 77 on the board, and with Viv and Greg heading their batting, realistically, I never thought we'd bowl them out for less. But I was hoping that we'd at least not go down without a whimper, at least make them earn their runs. That was reflected in what I said before we went out on the field.

> Kim Hughes: We were all gathered together in a tight bunch at the dressing room door and Bacchus first talked about how disappointed he was, and how we'd let the team and the crowd down. Then he said, 'When I was a young bloke I lost eleven tin soldiers ... well I fucken found 'em today! I'm expecting you blokes to get in there and do something.'

Marsh and nine other players knew that nothing short of a miracle could save them from ignominious defeat. Marsh continued on with his rallying speech to focus the team on saving face: 'There's a big crowd here, let's not let them down. Let's go out and try and get five or six of them out ...'

... But he never quite got to finish that speech.

Dennis Lillee always changed in the back of the dressing room, so he was at the rear of the group when his captain spoke from the doorway. Angrily he cut in, shouting, 'Make 'em fight for it, be buggered. We're going to beat these bastards!' And he stormed right past Marsh to lead the side out onto the ground.

That aggression and ironclad will and belief would carry through to Lillee's first over, which would go down as one of the most remarkable in the history of limited-overs, if not any, cricket.

Demon Dennis

Dennis Lillee

If only you could have been there to see it! The 'birth' of
one of the greats. It was the Gabba, on 1 November 1969.
Queensland had skittled WA for just 187 and there was a bit
of embarrassment in the camp over that. A young chap, not
long turned twenty, measured out his run at the Stanley Street
end. He strode and he strode, before finally stopping and care-
fully placing a marker at his feet. Tentatively, he looked down
the long runway and saw a figure crouched over his bat—the
veteran Sam Trimble, a fixture in the Queensland side for some
time. Play! A deep breath. And the long, mesmeric approach
began. We all took a deep breath, too.

Dennis Lillee's first ball in a first-class game for WA. We'd
seen enough of him to have high expectations. Arms and legs
whirling, he leapt into the air a long way from the popping
crease, landed lightly and fired one down at the waiting Trimble.
Not bad. Bit wayward. But quick. Very quick. And following

through down the wicket, close to Sam—flicking bits of sweat at his boots. And offering us all the first glimpse of the 'Lillee glare'. All this from a raw first-gamer—this incredible fire in his belly. Staring down Sam Trimble, for goodness sake. Thirty-five and a seasoned veteran! Lillee went on to get Trimble out, then one more wicket in that innings, and one in the second. A total of 22 overs for 3 wickets. Nothing to set the world on fire, but plenty to catch the eye.

Sitting down for a coldie in the dressing room after play that first night, the talk behind the hands among the veterans was, 'reckon we've got one here'. And we weren't the only ones to be taking notes during that game. Next thing, Ray Lindwall, one of Australia's very best speedsters, is down at the ground watching, and wanting to have a chat with the youngster. He takes Lillee upstairs to the Cricketers Club lounge, and throws him some pointers. 'Lindy' tells the kid he thinks his run-up might be a bit too long, and that his wide-angled approach would be better brought around to a straighter line in to the delivery leap. Then invites him and a couple of his teammates (the author included) out to his home for a barbecue. And a bit more of a one-on-one. Pretty impressive. For a lad playing his first really serious game.

Well, it seems that Lindy must have got on the phone to his old Australian opening partner, 'Nugget', down in Sydney after that. Because at our very next game, at the SCG, when play was over and we were traipsing from our dressing room past the members' bar towards the home team's room for a beer, a command came from among a group standing at the bar. 'Oi! Come here.' The unmistakable gravelly tones of Keith Miller. Looking straight at the new WA bowler.

Dennis Lillee never did make it to the NSW dressing room for drinks and a talk that night. Instead, he stood in awe, nervous as a kitten—and listened—while he got the once-over from another of Australian cricket's all-time greats. It was like a layer of cream on a cake for the young player. He'd made an impression, alright.

Lindwall and Miller! What an opening partnership they were. Lindy gliding in and rolling them out at good pace, swinging it left and right. Nugget, off a short run and explosive at the crease, fairly making the batsman dance. Lillee, perhaps a bit of a mixture of the two in the early stages of his career. Later, the refined version would perhaps lean more to Lindwall's control and movement of the ball.

There would be many more casual meetings with the two legends and, in the case of Lindy, a steady flow of letters offering advice. Like a good student, Lillee would continue to listen and to learn. As that first season continued, he blossomed. His second-innings return of 7–36 against South Australia in Perth added to a wonderful summer's haul of 32 wickets at 22.03. Which earned him a place in the Australian second team for a tour of New Zealand at season's end. A star had been born … *and how!*

'Run, Dennis. Run!' The words rang out loud at a suburban park in Perth. The words of Lillee's maternal grandfather, Len Halifax, a trainer of boxers who knew only too well the value of superb physical fitness. He knew that, grinding towards the end of a bout, if boxers didn't have 'stamina', no matter how much determination rested in their brains and in their hearts, they would be vulnerable—almost helpless—against an opponent who still had some pep in his step. Costly mistakes are made in the ring when the lungs and the limbs won't respond.

'Pop' Halifax, a short and wiry chap with worry wrinkles etched into his face, called it 'the second wind'. He would make a priceless gift to his young grandson when he imbued in him the need to work hard, every day if necessary, to be able to go to the well and draw on that wonderful asset. His dictum to Lillee was, 'If you can get your second wind and be in control of your body, then your mind will be free to cope with the job ahead.' It wasn't easy to start with, because the young Lillee had suffered from birth with weak ankles. Often in those days when he broke into a trot he'd simply fall over, and his parents were advised to obtain special boots that rose high above the ankles and that could be laced up tightly to provide the necessary support. In time the strength came, and he was able to put those boots away forever and answer a grandfather's call to *run*.

Throughout Lillee's illustrious career, that clarion call drove him to make a contribution to fitness every day, come rain, hail or sweltering sunshine—be it bowling a good stint or going for a punishing run. When wet weather stopped play he would put on a pair of shorts and run through the puddles, shrugging off the derisive hoots from teammates sheltering from the weather in the dressing room. As a result of this driving ambition to always be able to find the second wind, he was more often than not just as deadly in his final over of the day as he had been in the first. The great West Indian Viv Richards would attest to that, having watched Lillee fire off the final delivery of the day in a Test at the MCG, only to have it crash through Richards's defences and disturb the wooden trinity.

Of course there was more—much more—than consistent high levels of fitness to the truly great bowler that Dennis Lillee would become. Taken from the book *The Art of Fast Bowling*, which I co-wrote with Dennis and which was published in 1978, the 'assets for a fast bowler' were listed in the following order by a plebiscite of sixteen of the world's best pace bowlers of the day (the figure in brackets at the end of each row are how Dennis himself rated them at the time):

1. Stamina and physical fitness (2)
2. Ability to achieve express speed (1)
3. Ability to 'think a batsman out' (4)
4. Ability to swing the ball readily (5)
5. 'Killer' instinct (3)
6. Ability to bowl a good bouncer and yorker (6)
7. Good fieldsmen, particularly slips and wicketkeeper (8)
8. Ability to cut the ball off the wicket (10)
9. A fast bouncy wicket (9)
10. An astute and understanding captain (7)

No surprise that Dennis rated 'killer' instinct higher on the list than his contemporaries. That fired-up attitude was then—and would remain—so much a part of the Lillee package. Having followed his career closely, as a teammate then as a writer and broadcaster, I would elevate the ranking of 'ability to cut the ball off the wicket'. His performance in England in 1981 (when he battled illness to play the Tests, yet still took 39 wickets at 22.31), was based on a shortened run-up (to conserve energy), wonderful control of line and length and magnificent movement off the wicket.

But for me the word missing from the list is 'Will'—the ability of a bowler to impose his will on a situation. Dennis Lillee had oodles of this. So many times he dug deep and found that resolve. I have already mentioned the time he crashed through Viv Richards with the last ball of a long, hot day at the

MCG. And there would be no better indication of his towering will than in The Miracle Match. His ability to say, and believe, 'I can do it' and 'we can win this game' when he walked on the field staring defeat in the face.

A shining example for me of Dennis Lillee's will was during the 1975 World Cup in England—sitting in the bleachers at Leeds, watching a vital opening game against Pakistan slip away from Australia. We had posted a target of 278. But Asif Iqbal and Wasim Raja were cruising at 4–181 with plenty of overs to spare. Almost in desperation Ian Chappell threw the ball to Lillee. You could almost read the word 'will' over the start of his run-up for the *first* ball of the spell. It was into Asif's stumps before his bat had reached the bottom of its swing. That one delivery was the game-changer. Pakistan was dismissed for 205 and Lillee's figures from 12 overs were 5–34!

Perhaps Jeff Thomson, who partnered Lillee with such devastating effect, sums up this thing called 'will' the best:

> He never thought anything was impossible. Not that I didn't think the same. Just that I was a bit laid-back, whereas out on the field he was never laid-back. He always wanted to win. With me it was a bit more that I needed a reason to really fire up. If you didn't give me a reason I'd be a bit of a sleeping tiger. If Dennis sensed that, he used to wind me up.

Others had their own take on what drove Lillee to be so competitive, to be able so regularly to impose his will on a game situation.

> Viv Richards: I can only have respect for him. He was a Trojan. No matter what the circumstances—the wicket or the weather—he would always get something out of

it … he was the best fast bowler I ever encountered— for aggression, for never-say-die attitude, for being the most troublesome individual to me. Regardless of how much you might have thought you were 'in', you knew he would always think he could get you out. There was only one Dennis Lillee. You can't find another.

Rod Marsh: When I first stood at the other end to Dennis in a game for WA he was as raw as a carrot still in the ground, intent on doing just one thing and that was bowling every ball as fast as he could. On top of his great ability as a bowler was his contribution to team performance off the field. He was an inspiration to the seasoned campaigners as well as all the young fellows. He was so dedicated—and he tried so hard—that it was impossible to not be in there fighting with him.

Mick Malone: Whenever you had him in your side you felt as though you had a chance of winning. His work ethic was just faultless. He never left a stone unturned in his quest to become the best—and to stay the best.

Craig Serjeant:. No-one trained harder than Dennis … no-one bowled more balls in the nets … and when training was over he would go and do some running.

Bruce Yardley: Inspirational! He had this fierce desire. One: To be the best; and two: To take his team to victory. Team was just about everything to him.

Bruce Laird: One time during World Series Cricket in the West Indies he bowled and bowled to the point where he just blacked out. Still he wouldn't stop. The word 'quit' just wasn't in his vocabulary.

It was very early in his career for WA that Lillee received the nickname that has travelled with him ever since. Initially he copped 'Falcon'—a crude reference to the shape of his nose, when viewed side-on. But that was overtaken by 'FOT', thanks to his captain Tony Lock, with some help from a sharp-witted John Inverarity. In his first season for WA, Lillee was as green as the lush outfield grass of the WACA Ground. One day he was directed by Lock to tread from one side to the other at fine leg, while there was a left-hand–right-hand batting combination. Tired of having to constantly remind the forgetful young quickie that he must change sides when the batsmen changed ends, Lock let out with a loud whistle and screamed in his best Cockney accent, 'Come on Lil … you're like a fucking old tart!' Whereupon Inverarity, spectating from his position in the slips, seized on the initials of his captain's quaint epithet—so 'FOT' it was and still is.

A little green he may have been, but as the days of the 1970–71 season rolled by his name was gaining more and more clout, and it was no surprise when he was chosen for the Sixth Test against England. It was in Adelaide, rarely a wicket to favour the men of pace. With his mate Rod Marsh camped behind the stumps in the first innings, Lillee fired down 28.3 overs for figures of 5–84. A stellar beginning. Yet it wouldn't be until the first innings of the Seventh Test, at the SCG, that the scorers would write for the first time in a Test match the magical words 'Caught Marsh, Bowled Lillee'. John Hampshire was the first victim.

On the 'old' WACA wicket, so renowned for its pace and bounce, it was often better for a fast bowler on day two than it had been on the opening day. Lillee gave some sort of credence to this on 11 December 1971. It was the second day of an unofficial Test against a 'Rest of the World' side that had been cobbled together when a planned tour by South Africa was scrubbed. Australia had batted first and scored 349. At that stage there were no signs of what was to come—one of Dennis Lillee's finest hours. He arrived at the ground for the second day feeling unwell, claimed 2 wickets in his first 4 overs, and then asked Ian Chappell if he could have a spell. 'Give me one more,' was the skipper's request. What then transpired was quite extraordinary. As it happened, at the same time WA was in the field at the MCG, playing a Shield game against Victoria, with a fair crowd in. We kept hearing these roars from the other side of the boundary that had nothing to do with what was happening out on our ground. Then we took a wicket and couldn't wait to ask the incoming batsman what it was all about. 'Lillee's on fire in Perth,' we were told.

No wonder those in the MCG crowd with transistor radios were going bananas—Lillee was tearing through the classy opposition line-up. In the space of fifteen deliveries he bagged six more wickets—for innings figures of 8–29. His victims Sunil Gavaskar, Farokh Engineer, Clive Lloyd, Tony Greig, the great Gary Sobers (for a duck), Richard Hutton, Intikhab Alam and Bob Cunis. Chappell enforced the follow-on and Lillee claimed Engineer again, for a total of 9 wickets in the pre-lunch session. His figures for the game were 12–92, from 21.1 overs.

A month later Lillee was stopped in his tracks the last day of the fourth international against the Rest of the World. At the end of a follow-through there was a stabbing pain near the base of his spine. Subsequent X-rays drew a blank. Given a short rest—and thinking the problem may have been behind him—Lillee headed off on the 1972 tour of England. But in the nets before the first game the pain returned. He was taken to a specialist who applied manipulation under general anaesthetic, and Lillee proceeded through the five-Test series bagging 31 wickets—at the time a record for an Australian in an Ashes series in England.

Back home again in Australia, Lillee faced a gruelling summer of cricket. Five Sheffield Shield games and one for WA against the touring Pakistan side—between 4 November and 18 December. In that short space of time he bowled a mountainous total of 207 (eight-ball) overs. Then it was straight into a three-Test series against the Pakistanis. Bowling in the first innings of the Third, at the SCG in January, his back collapsed. With an enormous shooting pain up his spine, Lillee bowled out the game at little more than medium pace. The following month, during the Australian tour to the West Indies, Lillee finally received a diagnosis for his back problem when former West Indies first-class cricketer turned radiologist, Rudi Webster, offered to help. After a long series of X-rays was taken, Webster found three tiny fractures on two of the lumbar vertebrae, and suggested exercises to strengthen the back and stomach muscles. Lillee followed that advice, played only in the Jamaica Test, without taking a wicket, and went home seriously wondering, where to from here?

Home again, and things moved quickly. A Perth orthopaedic surgeon recommended full immobility. Lillee was encased in plaster from his buttocks to the top of his chest, and for six weeks went through hell. Then the plaster was hacked away, replaced with a ribbed harness that offered him some movement (and which could be removed for abluting), while he contemplated his future. Lillee decided not to try to play first-class cricket the following summer, 1973–74. Instead he took on the role of captain-coach at his club (Perth) and spent most of the summer improving his batting and strategic skills. He bowled in the back half of the season, but never at anywhere near full pace, taking the opportunity to develop a variety of deliveries that would benefit him later in his career, when raw pace was a thing of the past.

The winter of 1974 was a period of serious preparation. Working in tandem with Dr Frank Pyke at the University of WA, Lillee plunged into a series of isometric exercises aimed at further strengthening the stomach and back muscles, to better support the spine. They relied on a partner (me) to hold firm while a 'push' position was established and held. In the beginning I was able to do the 'hold' part with ease. By the time we embarked on an eastern states tour to start the new season, I had my feet against motel walls and still couldn't hold him!

These exercises were backed by a killing running program. Lillee was fitter and stronger than ever, but could he recapture the magic with the ball in his hand? The first trial was South Australia in Adelaide where he bagged 7 wickets for the game. With that comeback performance under his belt, the selectors named Jeff Thomson and him to lead the attack against the touring England team in the upcoming First Test in Brisbane. Between them, the duo would rack up 13 wickets as Australia went on to win. 'Lillian Thomson' had been born.

The duo would team up magnificently for the first five Tests and blitz the England batting. It was devastating stuff. This partnership of pace—Thomson's blistering speed, combined with Lillee's mastery of the finer points—would last for twenty-three Tests in tandem. A total of 197 wickets, 106 of them coming from Lillee, 91 from Thomson. That's 8.6 wickets per Test, and most of them up-the-order bats.

With or without Jeff Thomson at the other end, Dennis Lillee would continue to strut the world stage, and rightfully earn the reputation of the world's best. For me the crowning glory came early in 1977, when, between 1 January and 16 March, he registered three ten-wicket matches in Tests: 10–135 against Pakistan at the MCG; 11–123 against New Zealand in Auckland; and 11–165 in the Centenary Test against England at the MCG. In the five Tests he played in that period, his combined figures were a stunning 41 wickets for 750 runs. All in the shadow of the formation of World Series Cricket—a development in which Lillee was one of the catalysts. Present at an informal gathering in a Perth hotel, Lillee complained about how little money players were getting out of the game, suggesting that perhaps a made-for-television series could help in the players' bid for a bigger slice of the cake. The idea was put to media magnate Kerry Packer and from this WSC was born.

Worn out by his travails in the Australian summer, Lillee chose not to go on the 1977 tour of England, during which news of WSC hit the media. Along with the rest of the troupe, Lillee rode out the storm, and in fifteen WSC Supertests he bagged 79 wickets at 22.5, close to his career Test average of 23.92. And you could argue that those WSC wickets were harder to come by than the 355 he captured in official Test matches—such was the quality of the West Indies and World XI batting depth. Now add four internationals against the Rest of the World and those fifteen Supertests to his 70 Tests and his grand total is 458 victims from 89 games, average 23.72, rate 5.15 per game. That would place him sixth in the all-time rankings (for wickets taken) with a strike rate second only to Muttiah Muralitharan:

	Games	Wickets	Average	Wickets/game
M. Muralitharan (S.L.)	133	800	22.72	6.02
S. Warne (Aust.)	145	708	25.41	4.88
A. Kumble (India)	132	619	29.65	4.69
G. McGrath (Aust.)	124	563	21.64	4.54
C. Walsh (W.I.)	132	519	24.44	3.93
D. Lillee (Aust.)	89	458	23.72	5.15

Beyond WSC there were more high points for the champion of pace. A more refined action, featuring a shorter, more rhythmic approach, would produce many good days. In the 1981 tour to England, despite an attack of viral pneumonia, he managed 39 wickets at 22.31, including 11 wickets in his final Test appearance in England, the Sixth, at The Oval. He would have one more ten-wicket match (which included his best single-innings return of 7–83) in the First Test against the West Indies (1981–82), played at by far his most productive Test match venue, the MCG.

In all of his 70 Tests, he would capture ten or more wickets in a match seven times, plus twenty-three times an innings of five or more wickets. Incidentally, it was during that game against the West Indies at the MCG that he broke the world record for Test wickets (previously held by West Indian spinner Lance Gibbs at 309)—Larry Gomes, caught by Greg Chappell at first slip. The batsman most dismissed by Lillee in Tests was England's Alan Knott (twelve times), followed by four on nine—Viv Richards and England's Dennis Amiss, John Edrich and

Graham Gooch. And he would have the distinction of taking a wicket with his final delivery in Tests, the Third against Pakistan at the SCG in 1984.

Yet the headlines weren't all positive for the fiery speedster. In 1977 he caused a bit of a scandal during the Centenary Test at the MCG when the players lined up to meet the Queen. When it came his turn to meet Her Majesty, Lillee pulled out an auto-graph book and asked for her signature. Naturally she politely refused. It simply wasn't done, to ask for an autograph in this manner, and it caused quite a stir at the time. Some time later, though, an autographed a photo of the incident arrived in the mail at his home in Perth!

He also became involved in the manufacture and marketing of an aluminium cricket bat, an exercise that ended up ruffling a few feathers. At the WACA Ground in December 1979 he brought the controversial bat out during an Ashes Test, and it wasn't long before England captain Mike Brearley complained to the umpire that the bat was damaging the ball. There followed a scene out of a Keystone Kops movie. There were no rules against the use of such a bat, but Greg Chappell sent twelfth man Rod Hogg out with a selection of wooden bats. Which Lillee rejected. After a lot of to-ing and fro-ing Lillee gave in, with one parting gesture—mightily throwing the offending bat towards the pavilion. It was an unseemly event, which halted play for some 10 minutes. But I couldn't help thinking that the English wooden bat–makers may have had a say in the pro-testations that day against the Dennis Lillee 'Combat'! Which recorded brisk sales in the ensuing weeks.

Further controversy for Lillee (and his mate Rod Marsh) came on the unhappy 1981 England tour. During the Third Test at Leeds, Australia were in command and forced the follow-on. The ground bookmakers showed odds of 500–1 on an England victory. Noting this, the pair had a third party place small bets as a bit of a joke. Then, against those odds, England went on to win the game. A scandal erupted when the two players pocketed a few thousand pounds along with their team's defeat.

There was another, rather unsavoury, incident when Lillee clashed with the Pakistani batsman Javed Miandad during the First Test at the WACA Ground (1981–82). Miandad was a scratchy individual, whose high-pitched voice and on-field antics did not easily endear him to opponents. He ran a Lillee delivery down behind square leg and collided with the bowler, standing in his follow-through position, during his run. According to Greg Chappell, there was a combination of Lillee getting in the batsman's way *and* Miandad jabbing Lillee with his bat in the process of the collision. Things turned nasty when Lillee made a half-playful kick at Miandad with his boot. The Pakistani responded by raising his bat, as if to strike Lillee with it. Fists up … bat in the air … and umpire Tony Crafter in between like a boxing referee, breaking it up. There were wild calls for blood from the media, and others. The matter was considered by Lillee's teammates, who applied a fine of $200. This was overruled by the Australian authorities, who reduced the fine to $120, but added a two-match ban (for two one-day internationals).

Thankfully, the good far outweighed the not-so-good and Dennis Lillee retired a national hero in January 1984. He had served his country (and his state and clubs) magnificently, and it was time to put away the boots.

Quite early in his international career, Lillee had set the tone with the following comment: 'Batsmen are like thieves to me, desperately trying to steal from me the ascendancy I believe is mine. And I treat them like faceless, meaningless thieves.' But, above all, this was a great team man ... who readily gave to the cause. Who would, having bowled his heart out, don a pair of shorts and a T-shirt and go across to the nets to work on their technique with the likes of Mick Malone, Terry Alderman and me. A man who, along with his mate Rod Marsh, would often contrive to break the tension in the dressing room by perpetrating some ridiculous act. Who would set out to make his first ball of the day his best of day—and his last ball equally as good! And at the end of the day, more often than not, he'd flop onto the seat in front of his locker and remove his boots to reveal socks bright red with blood around the toe area.

In his retirement years Dennis Lillee has earned a lofty reputation as one of the world's premier pace-bowling coaches. Countless players, both in Australia and elsewhere, have benefitted from his wonderful analytical and remedial skills. Just ask Mitchell Johnson who it was who put his game back on the rails and led to a purple patch of form against England in the 2013–14 season, then in South Africa shortly afterwards! Lillee has also given back to his home state, with a long spell as president of the Western Australian Cricket Association. But it's as 'Dennis the Menace', the world-champion fast bowler, that he'll be best remembered, along with the strains of *'Li-lee ... Li-lee ... Li-lee ...'* wafting over the ground as the champ got to the top of his mark.

Master Blaster

Viv Richards

It's hard to argue against the fact that the players who get us sitting on the edge of our seats at a cricket game are the thumping hitters. They provide the real pyrotechnics of the game. While it's true that there are pace merchants—sending the ball rearing over the wicketkeeper's head and one bounce into the sightscreen—who can bring the crowd to its feet. And spin whizzes—pitching in the rough outside leg stump and hitting the top of off—who can leave spectators with their jaws on the floor. The Jeff Thomsons and the Shane Warnes. But it's the arrival at the crease of a bruising big hitter that really stirs our juices and fuels our expectation.

In my time and experience, three stand out, in chronological order—England's Colin ('Ollie') Milburn, Viv Richards and Adam Gilchrist. And legend suggests that, before my time, the Englishman Gilbert Jessop with a bat in hand was also something to behold.

Milburn was a pocket battleship. Weighing in at a hefty 18 stone (115 kilograms) from below-average height. With a heavyweight's set of forearms and cracking wrists, he used every gram of that bulk to hit the ball as hard and as far as any. Though such a hefty smiter of the ball, Milburn was no slogger. The man played with close to a copybook technique. Operating almost exclusively from a half-step forward, he was able to comfortably dispatch short-pitched deliveries to either side of the wicket through immense power in his forearms and breaking wrists. There was little fuss about Milburn's power, no sense of an atomic bomb going off.

He played nine Tests and turned out for WA in 1966–67 and 1968–69, and for me one innings stands out. Playing in Adelaide he belted a century in 77 minutes, with sixteen fours and a six. I batted with Ollie that day and scored just two in a partnership of 60, spectating in awe from the non-striker's end as he put on an amazing fire show. Because of an arrangement with his English bat-maker, that summer Milburn was supplied with as many bats as he needed. He'd just take one out of the wrapper and put it straight to use against a brand new ball out in the middle. So hard did he hit them that, at the end of any sort of a stay at the crease, the face of the bat would be splintered and he'd have a new one brought out. That season he'd have gone close to double figures—in new bats, that is. I shudder to think how far he would have hit them using today's product, which needs none of the rolling in, oiling and battering of the old days. Same weight. But chock-full of vibrant life.

In the summer of 1968 Milburn lit up Lord's in the second Ashes Test. He came in at the fall of the first wicket on the first day and was out before lunch for 83. His devastating stroke play drew a standing ovation from the staid Lord's turnout. But there *were* mutterings that one just didn't play that way in a Test match … especially at the home of cricket!

Back with WA, in Brisbane in November 1968 (when I was living in England), he dawdled along to be 61 at lunch, before unleashing an astonishing display of power hitting—adding 181 off his own bat in the two-hour afternoon session. Sadly, not always do good things last forever. Soon after finishing that season for WA and returning to England, Milburn suffered the loss of an eye in a car accident, virtually ending his career. At the age of 48 he succumbed to a heart attack. In truth, Ollie was plain ahead of his time.

Though no less a brutal hitter, Viv Richards was renowned more for explosive power and, at times, for his unorthodoxy. But much more on him shortly.

Next, to the man they called the 'Croucher', because of his unusual stance. Gilbert Jessop, who played over the turn of the twentieth century, stood a similar height to Milburn, but was little over half his weight. Yet it is reported that he hit the ball just as hard and far, with an extraordinary range of strokes. From crashing drives, cuts and pulls to delicate glides and glances, at his best Jessop would score at 100 runs an hour. In 1900 he scored 157 in an hour against the West Indian team, but he is best known for a match-winning century in the 1902 Oval Test against Australia. Going in at a parlous 5–48, he took to the Australians and scored 104 out of 139 runs scored while he was at the crease, reaching his century in 77 minutes. Measured by time at the crease, not today's method of balls faced, this remains the second-fastest Test century of all time. A true titan of power batting!

Talk about taking the long handle to the bowling! That was the hallmark of the amazing big hitting of Adam Gilchrist.

Considerably taller than the other trio under examination, he held the bat high on the handle and, employing lightning-fast reflexes combined with a plan to 'just hit the ball', he belted the bowling in all forms of the game. If there was a signature stroke among the complete array in his bag, perhaps it would be the short-arm pull through or over mid-wicket. With this stroke, anything a fraction short of a length was fruit for the sideboard. But here was a batsman whose eye was always on the ball, never the scoreboard. If it was there to be hit, he'd hit it.

While you could never call Gilly 'arrogant', one day in a Test match at Johannesburg he went awfully close—both to a measured degree of arrogance *and* to a bar of gold worth 1.3 million rand. His attempt to win gold by hitting an advertising hoarding 10 metres in the air and way over the mid-wicket boundary missed by less than a metre. He then regained his cool to go on and reach 200 from 212 deliveries.

The extraordinary force of his batting is underlined by a Test strike rate of 82 per 100 balls, and 96 from 100 in ODIs. His total of 33 centuries in Tests (17) and ODIs (16) is the highest by a 'keeper. And he's the only player to have hit 100 sixes in Tests. Numbers there to have Viv Richards bowing his head, though the West Indian holds, by one ball, the world record for the fastest Test century—he having faced 56 deliveries, compared with Gilly's 57 (against England in Perth in December 2006). Gilchrist consistently batted in Tests like others only dare to do in the short forms. Which were tailor-made for his rambunctious stroke-play. One memorable match, the 2007 World Cup final against Sri Lanka at Barbados, saw him hitting a lightning 149 off 104 balls (thirteen fours and eight sixes) and paving the way for an Australian victory. Another had him, playing for the Deccan Chargers in the T20 Indian Premier League in 2008, making 109 not out from 47 balls, with ten sixes.

Now to Viv. Well, he was different. And he certainly lived up to the name of 'Master Blaster'. He chose never to bow to a bowler. The reverse, in fact, is true—he set out from ball one to dominate. The better the bowler, the more determined he was to take the high ground. This resulted in some titanic tussles—as both Dennis Lillee and Jeff Thomson, plus many others, would attest. Viv was a Grade A risk-taker, which meant that early in an innings the bowler felt he had a chance. A small window of opportunity.

Standing behind the stumps for Australia, Rod Marsh was in a good position to observe:

> Quite often he would come out swinging and his first twenty or so runs would be high risk, unlike, say, the way Greg Chappell would start an innings. That meant you had a real chance with him early on. Then he'd start to bat properly and that's when you knew you were in deep shit. And it wouldn't necessarily be a long day, because he scored so quickly.

Dennis Lillee, too, understood:

> His tactic would be to go for you early on, trying to get on top. If he got to 20 or 25 he seemed to think, 'Now I can bat properly.' Then you knew you were in a bit of trouble.

Legend has it that Viv gave some thought to trying himself out as a boxer. He certainly had the build for it. And his early nickname 'Smoky' was a direct reference to the American heavyweight champ, 'Smokin' Joe' Frazier. In the end, cricket won out, and that extraordinary musculature was one element in Viv's ability to spank the ball almost out of sight.

The other element lay in *attitude*. Which Viv had in spades. He simply loved to smack the bowling. During the 1975–76 tour to Australia he made a big century in a tour match against WA. Included were two strokes that stand out in my memory of that day. Batting at the northern end of the ground, he ran down to a spinner and gently eased the ball over the long-off fence, over a high wall and into the street in front of the police building. Now that's a very big hit. (But it did have the benefit of the batsman's forward motion.) Later, a shot to better it. This time standing at the southern end—to the same spinner—he rocked forward on release, then got the length and rocked back. From a position of no forward momentum whatsoever, he used his massive forearms to thrash the ball into a grandstand some 15 metres beyond the long-on boundary. With the ball still going up when it clattered into the seats!

As good as that was, people who were present at Kensington Oval, Barbados in 1978—the day Jeff Thomson took on Viv Richards in a game when Clive Lloyd says he witnessed the fastest bowling he'd ever seen—still talk about that one particular stroke. In whispered tones. About a six that came out of this clash of the giants. Thommo to Viv. For both men it was Sydney or the bush. Viv skied a short one to square leg—and got away with it.

A monumentally peeved Thommo:

> Well, I thought I'd give him another short one—and I'd really let this one go. I bowled as hard as I could and he hit it as hard as I've ever seen a cricket ball hit. The ball came through about chest high and he pulled it

off his nose and it went about my height off the ground like a bullet out of a gun through square leg. There was a building over the boundary fence, not all that far at Kensington Oval, that looked something like a chicken coop. Well, the ball crashed into the roof of that so hard I thought it was going to knock the whole stand over. I thought, 'Bullshit!' Viv just rolled his eyes. I don't think he realised he could hit a ball so hard.

It was simply in Viv Richards's DNA. He chose to fight fire with fire. 'The faster and more evil they were, the more aggressive I tried to be.' All of which made him one of the game's great entertainers. When Viv was out there, something was either happening, or about to happen. People talk about technique. That the greatest of them all, Don Bradman, would play across the line. Well, Viv was recently voted the third best Test batsmen of all time, after Bradman and India's Sachin Tendulkar. And Viv also played across the line. Happily.

Often when I whipped the ball away to leg off my middle stump, the experts would suck in their breath, shake their heads and tell me I was hitting across the line. What is wrong with that when you consistently hit the ball for four? Bowlers would call me lucky. The more I did it, the luckier I became!

Dennis Lillee reckons it offered him a glimmer of hope.

I always thought I had a chance to bowl him out. He would try to work the ball a bit across the line into the leg side. Particularly early in his innings, I thought he was a bit of a chance with an outie.

Rod Marsh remembers the Australians working on Richards during the first year of World Series Cricket.

> We worked a plan to bowl wide of off stump and let him come after us. He did and we had a lot of success, because he always wanted to hit through the leg side. The second year we started that way … and he belted us through the off-side. What do you do then? Straighten up your line—and he belts you through the on-side.

While others pumped up the bodily protection from the late 1970s and early 1980s—donning helmets, arm guards, chest guards, you name it—Richards remained steadfast. He convinced himself that he didn't need the helmet.

> The fear of failure and losing was far greater than the fear of being hurt. I was aware of certain deliveries that went by close. That didn't frighten me … just kept me alert and alive. I actually enjoyed facing a really good fast bowler, even one who bowled good bumpers.

But occasionally he did pay a price. 'I sniffed the leather on a few occasions, especially in Australia, and it smelled very sweaty.'

Viv *was* different. When his team went in to bat he would watch the first few balls bowled, then pad up and go to sleep on the rubdown table. (For much of his time the Windies openers were Gordon Greenidge and Desmond Haynes, so he wasn't often called on early …) When it came time to go out, he would splash water on his face to fully wake up, grab a piece of chewing gum and head for the door, his mind clear of gremlins.

'This is now my war. Me and my chewing gum against the world.' How's that for cool! If you were lucky enough to be there at the ground as he walked out, you got a taste of the Viv swagger. Most loved it. Some thought it was too arrogant.

Jeff Thomson rises to his defence:

> People get the wrong impression of Viv, thinking he's a smart-arse because he walked with a real swagger. He was no different to Dennis—ego and all that—but without it you amount to nothing, you'll be nobody. But Viv, no helmet all those years. Wasn't a bad effort. We hit him on the head, but it didn't matter. He was just an inspiration to play with. I don't think you'd see too many blokes as dynamic as him. The Chris Gayles and the Kieron Pollards, mate they're not fit to do up Viv's bootlaces.

Greg Chappell would agree:

> Probably the best batsman of my era—in the way that he could change a game in a short space of time. I remember sending the West Indies in, in Adelaide. It had a bit of a green tinge to it—and I wasn't about to give their bowlers the advantage. Dennis Lillee and Lennie Pascoe opened the bowling and got an early wicket. Viv came in and Dennis bowled him two absolute jaffers, beat him all ends up. Then [Dennis] bowled him a bouncer, which just flicked the peak of his cap. Knocked it a little bit sideways. Dennis gave Viv the 'look'. You could read Viv's reaction. He put the cap back on straight, pulling it down tight. And looked back. Virtually saying 'Right, we've got a contest on

here.' Next ball he hit straight back over Dennis's head and he was 70-odd before lunch. And had changed the game. At a time when we could easily have had four or five wickets before lunch. He was almost more likely to get runs when the conditions were toughest.

No surprise, either, that the flamboyant Kim Hughes was a big fan:

> Viv had the ability and the power to decimate the bowling and, at the same time, make the batsman at the other end look, and feel, better. He stood alone, in that he could intimidate an attack. Viv saw it early and just belted it. You had to love his style and persona, the way he used to strut. He'd hit you out of the park, then go and arrogantly tap down the wicket.

Viv had all the shots and that little bit of extra time to play them, like most of the true champions. He goes down in history as one of the best players of pure pace bowling. And one of the best exponents of the hook shot of all time. (Just ask Jeff Thomson about Barbados.) Like many of the very best, his first move was on to the front foot. Then he would pick up the length. If it was short pitched, he had the ability and time to rock back and hammer the ball square of the wicket on either side. (Unlike Colin Milburn, who would cut, hook and pull off the front foot.) With Viv, there was a blend of timing and force. And, in much the same way as Glenn McGrath in his prime would announce before a series that he was targeting a particular batsman in the opposition, Viv's mission was to destroy the opposition's best fast bowler. And, of course, in achieving that aim, as he did so often, he rolled out a magic carpet for his teammates to ride on.

The archetypal big-match player who loved a challenge, who got kicks out of taking risks and helping himself to the bounty. There is a simple message in Richards's thinking about batting and batsmanship. 'What should be drilled into every player's head, as it was into mine, is shot selection.' All right for some. For the rest it isn't quite so simple.

Isaac Vivian Alexander Richards was born on 7 March 1952 in Antigua. From an early age, he was guided towards playing cricket by his father, Malcolm, who represented the island nation. Tirelessly, he would bowl to Viv and his younger brother, Mervyn, in the back yard of their home. Malcolm Richards was a guiding light in more ways than one. 'He convinced me that practice was more important than coaching.' That went as far as mirror batting, or shadow batting, taking the idea from Muhammad Ali.

His father was also quite religious and his beliefs meant that Malcolm wouldn't allow his sons to play any sport on Sundays. This was time in purgatory for Viv and Mervyn. One Sunday the pair decided they'd skip church to play an important game for their local cricket team. Inevitably, their father added two and two together and got four. As Viv reports, he laid into them when they got home. The boys took their punishment but made a case for future leniency. Compromise was reached—provided they went to church first, they could play after.

Viv grew up loving both cricket and soccer. He was able to happily spread himself between the two sports—until a cricket tour clashed with one for soccer. Cricket had a much better organised structure at the time and won the day. Lovers of the summer game would rejoice. Seventeen years old and playing his first game for Antigua, he set the unwanted record of being out three times without scoring a run in the same game … *and* causing a near-riot. The first ball he was given out, caught bat-pad, when he knew he hadn't hit it. The young tyro put on quite a show and spectators started jumping the fence to protest. Play was suspended. Oddly enough, Richards was reinstated and sent out to bat again. He was promptly stumped without scoring. In the second innings he was caught, again without scoring. As a result of his behaviour, he was banned from all cricket for two years. 'From being the golden boy, I was now in disgrace.' During the period of suspension he threw his energy into soccer, and boxing. His coach in the latter pursuit thought he had the ability to go on with it. But when the suspension came to an end, it was back to his first sporting battleground. Looking back later, Viv had no regrets. 'Fighting was hard, but not as hard as facing Dennis Lillee and Jeff Thomson.'

Back in the Antigua team, Richards began to make an impression, which resulted in an invitation to play club cricket in Somerset, with a view to advancing to the County side—a big adventure for a twenty-two-year-old. Which almost died before it began. When he arrived at Heathrow Airport, he didn't have the correct papers for entry, but after much discussion he was finally allowed in. At the end of the season he was offered a two-year contract with the County, and in 1974 a marvellous association began.

While at Somerset the young Richards came under the influence of captain Brian Close, a tough campaigner towards the end of a fine career that had begun with Yorkshire and England. 'He became something of a mentor to me. The perfect example at that stage of my development.' Richards was soon joined at Somerset by Ian Botham and Joel Garner, beginning a long golden era for a County which had been starved of success.

Richards forged a tight friendship with Botham—kindred spirits, and great cricketers. 'People used to say he was my white brother.' The pair even did a stage show together called 'The King and I'. And when Richards and Garner were inexplicably sacked by the County before the 1987 season, Botham quit in protest. 'It was a very big decision made by a very big man.'

At the conclusion of his first season with Somerset, Richards was chosen to tour India with the West Indies, and made his debut in the First Test at Bangalore. It was an inauspicious beginning, scoring just 4 and 3. But the twenty-two-year-old made a statement in the following Test, at Delhi, with a memorable unbeaten 192. 'My confidence was in tatters after the first Test, but I was determined I would not fail again.' This was no shy, retiring innings.

However, the spin of India was something very different from the ferocious pace of Dennis Lillee and Jeff Thomson that he faced in Australia in 1975–76. 'They were quick, very quick. Over after over.' This was a true baptism of fire, and he failed to even make a half-century in his first six innings. Team psychologist Rudi Webster isolated the problem as a lack of sustained concentration, and he slowly gained in confidence and finished the tour with plenty of runs.

During that time Richards proved to be one of the West Indies' heroes in winning the inaugural World Cup in 1975. The final against Australia at Lord's was an unforgettable clash. Batting first, West Indies made 8–291 from their allotted 60 overs—of which Viv had contributed only 5. However, when it came time for his team to take the field he ran out three Australians (Alan Turner, Ian and Greg Chappell). It was a masterly performance—and, as it turned out, a match-winning contribution. 'We had actually discussed this before the game and decided they weren't very good runners between the wickets, and that maybe we could pick up some of them that way.' Their pre-match analysis proved correct—the West Indies ran out five Australian batsmen to win by 17 runs that day. From that game on his opponents knew—if you took a run near Viv it was at your own peril. He developed into a brilliant all-round fielder and a wonderful slips catch, for years unrivalled in the infield 'ring'. The West Indies were able to win the following World Cup, in 1979, thanks this time to a Richards century in the final at Lord's.

If he'd endured some problems in Australia in the early stages of the 1975–76 tour, the calendar year of 1976 was the high point of Richards's stellar career—three Tests against Australia (in Australia), four against India (in the West Indies) and four against England (in England)—posting a record 1710 runs. He scored one century in Australia, three against the Indians and a century and two double-centuries in England. And the bar may have been set even higher, had he not been forced to miss the Lord's Test because of a bout of glandular fever. To make matters even worse, he had to spend the whole of that Test confined to his hotel room, for fear of spreading the germ to other players. Richards's mark stood for 30 years, before Pakistan's Mohammad Yousuf took it in 1988. Both had played in eleven Tests and had nineteen innings.

After the 1976 tour to England, Richards came to Australia to play for Queensland—and The Miracle Match.

> I was invited to join Jeff Thomson in an arrangement with the Brisbane radio station 4IP. Sadly I could only make limited appearances, because I had to leave

and return to the West Indies team for a series against Pakistan. But I did benefit greatly from my experience. I viewed the Australian cricket system—the way they performed and played—as the hardest I'd seen. To be asked to be part of that, it couldn't get any better for me. To be in that environment was a real privilege. I learnt a great deal. I am a competitor myself and to be in that highly competitive environment was a great educational process for me. At that stage I was still feeling my way around in Test cricket and to play with and against people like Greg Chappell and Jeff Thomson, who I admired tremendously, was just a wonderful experience.

Richards played four first-class games for the state, before being recalled to play for West Indies.

The Richards juggernaut gained momentum and rolled on ... and on. He was a dominant force in the World Series Cricket years (1977–79). Kerry Packer had gathered the cream of international cricket from right around the globe. Richards says the games were very competitive. 'There was huge prize money, with winner take all. There were no arrangements, no secret agreements. It was without doubt some of the toughest cricket I ever played.' In all, Viv appeared in fourteen Supertests, scoring 1281 runs at the average of 55.70. Only Greg Chappell produced better figures: from the same number of games, 1416 runs at 56.64. 'The three years were beautiful years. I would like to have done it officially, but it was not imperative.'

In 1981, England toured the West Indies and Richards made a century in the first Test ever played at his home ground of

St John's, Antigua. 'I would have to rank that innings right at the top of the pile of my most rewarding and satisfying innings.' (This was after local black magic practitioners had tried to use the occasion for their own ends, with threats to Viv and his family.) While this had been a patient, determined knock, five years later (same ground, same opponent) he posted the fastest Test 100 (in terms of balls faced). Reaching 50 in 34 balls, the century 22 balls later. Ask him, though, what was his most memorable innings and he'll tell you it was against India at Sabina Park in Jamaica in February 1983. The home side was left an hour plus 20 overs to score 172 to win. To Richards's delight, the batsmen were given a licence to 'go ballistic'. Dismissing the handicap of an injured thumb, he belted 61 off 36 balls (four sixes and five fours) and then watched as his team won in the last over.

The 1984–85 tour of Australia heralded the end of Clive Lloyd's reign as captain and Viv was named his replacement. His last series as skipper was 1990–91 against Australia at home and his undefeated series record as captain was maintained with a 2–1 win. Richards captained the West Indies in 50 Test matches from 1984–1991 (for twenty-seven wins and fifteen losses). He is the only West Indies captain never to lose a series, defeating England and Australia (both at home and away) and India and New Zealand at home. As captain he had to learn to be more tolerant. His tenure was, however, not without controversy. One incident was an aggressive, 'finger-flapping' appeal leading to the incorrect dismissal of England batsman Rob Bailey in the Barbados Test in 1990—described by *Wisden* as 'at best undignified and unsightly … at worst calculated gamesmanship'.

Viv Richards stands proudly shoulder-to-shoulder with the very best the game has seen. Here's a sample of how he ranks among the greats:

In 2000, he was voted one of the five Cricketers of the Century—along with Sir Donald Bradman, Sir Garfield Sobers, Sir Jack Hobbs and Shane Warne.

In 2002, he was judged by *Wisden* as having played the best ODI innings of all time—189 not out against England at Old Trafford in 1984.

In 2002, he was chosen by *Wisden* as the greatest ODI batsman of all time—as well as the third-greatest Test batsman of all time, after Sir Don Bradman and Sachin Tendulkar.

In the International Cricket Committee (ICC) all-time rankings for the best batsmen in Tests he is currently ranked at equal sixth after Sir Donald Bradman, Sir Len Hutton, Sir Jack Hobbs, Ricky Ponting and Peter May.

In the ICC's all-time ODI rankings he is currently number one, followed by Zaheer Abbas and Ian Chappell.

In 2004, a poll by American television giant ESPN, participated in by fifteen of the leading names in cricketing history, voted Richards the third greatest-ever player after Bradman and Sobers, and the second greatest-ever batsman after Bradman. He was also voted the greatest cricketer since 1970, ahead of Ian Botham and Shane Warne.

In 2006, in a study done by a team at ESPN's *Cricinfo* magazine, Richards was again chosen the greatest ODI batsman ever.

In Tests he scored 8540 runs in 121 matches at an average of 50.23 (including twenty-four centuries). Combine those figures with his statistics from fourteen games in World Series Cricket: A total of 135 games, 9821 runs at 50.89.

He remains one of only four non-English cricketers to have scored 100 first-class centuries, the others being Sir Donald Bradman, New Zealander Glenn Turner and Pakistani Zaheer Abbas.

In an ODI against New Zealand at Dunedin in 1987 he scored 119 and took 5–41—the only man to achieve this ODI 'double'.

In 1994 he was appointed an Officer of the Order of the British Empire (OBE) for services to cricket, and in 1999 he was made a Knight of the Order of the National Hero (KNH) by his native country, Antigua and Barbuda.

If nothing else, Viv Richards is a man of high principle. He has spoken out about the practice of sledging (players using abusive language and gestures against each other on the field) and has railed against instances of what he called 'racism' in the sport. His reputation was enhanced in certain quarters when he refused a 'blank-cheque' offer to play for a rebel West

Indies squad in South Africa during the apartheid era. He did so twice—in 1983 and again in 1984.

After all was said and done, the great Viv Richards acknowledged that the hardest and most satisfying Test cricket was against the Australians. 'For them winning is everything.' And he rates Dennis Lillee as the most dangerous fast bowler he ever faced. Their careers collided and produced some real fireworks—Lillee the arch aggressor with the ball, Richards an equal opposing force with the bat. Two massive personalities. Lillee of the flowing mane, shirt buttoned low to reveal a hairy chest and jangling gold chain, plus those menacing follow-throughs right down the track, invading the batsman's space. Viv of the boxer's physique, the chest-out swagger and the constant chew on gum. You couldn't have written a more gripping script than when the two met out in the middle. And the punters would flock to bear witness.

> Viv: [Lillee] was always pretty accurate with his line and if you missed his bouncer you were hit. What is more, he never bowled a short ball without a reason. Not that he or anyone else discouraged me from hooking. I felt that when I was batting against a notorious fast bowler and hit a ball sweetly for six, it was a special shot. It was a way of taming that bully.

As for Lillee himself:

> I always looked forward to bowling to Viv. I never worried, never had a sleepless night, if the game was coming up or an innings was approaching. But I was always aware that with both of us, it would be a case of 'me or you'.

For Richards and Lillee the battle was about to begin again. Lillee charged onto the field at the WACA Ground, leading his team still reeling from the morning's play. Viv walked onto the pitch with his usual swagger—a 77-run target, and Dennis Lillee, in his sights.

Head-on collision

After the short lunch break the spectators at the WACA Ground returned to their seats, the tension having seemingly built rather than diminished following WA's performance with the bat. They were eager to see what local hero Dennis Lillee could now do with the ball.

> Wayne Clark: I [had] looked out at the crowd after our innings ended and noticed that a lot of them were leaving the ground. I couldn't blame anybody for doing that … But they must have just gone for a walk, or something, to get over what they'd seen, because after the Queensland innings began the crowd just got bigger and bigger.

Queensland's captain, Greg Chappell, sensed that something was coming:

> The Lillee–Richards bout promised to be a real battle of the game's heavyweights. Dennis was in his prime, he

had this green and bouncy wicket and the Fremantle Doctor at his back ... and Viv was a rising champion. It was going to be on for young and old.

Television commentator Bob Simpson sensed it, too:

If WA are going to get up at all it'll be through the strong right arm of Dennis Lillee. This is a test of supremacy— Dennis Lillee is still considered the best bowler in the world and Viv Richards the best bat. Prestige is at stake and when two greats clash there's going to be a result somewhere along the line. I think this is going to be the most absorbing part of the afternoon.

And Daryl Foster, WA squad co-ordinator:

I've never known Dennis to be so angry in a game. I remember sitting next to him in the dressing room and he was going crook about 'the batsmen giving their wickets away' ... Then, when it came time to go out and bowl ... I knew that white line fever was only a breath away!

Richards and Lillee first came face to face during the West Indies 1975–76 tour of Australia. Lillee missed the fourth of the six Tests in the series—yet from nine innings claimed the West Indian four times, twice clean bowled. It was a convincing beginning for the Australian, who, over their careers in Tests and WSC Supertests, would win the day sixteen times—more than his record against any other batsman. That statistic tells a story about Lillee's ability to lift against the best. From his positive start against Richards in a West Indies cap the previous summer, Dennis knew this. So did Viv. The clash between the two *was* pivotal to WA's remote chances of getting into a game that had been nigh-on thrown away by its batsmen. Lillee would need to dominate Richards again. And with such a low score to protect, he needed to do it fast.

Alan Jones, Viv Richards's opening partner, was sure that Lillee would be right in the batsman's face, whoever it may be.

> I knew Dennis was fully fired up. During the lunch break he went across to the nets and when he came back he slammed their dressing room door so hard, I'm sure he broke it. He was verbally getting right up everyone in the WA room … and we were hearing it, from next door … I used to like taking the first ball, but as we walked out I said to Viv, 'You're on more money than me, you can face.'

The scene was set. Lillee, standing away in the distance at the River End. Off a very long run. Viv Richards, a lone figure standing at the striker's end, characteristically chewing on gum. The quickie straining at the leash. The batsman trying to give off an air of nonchalance. From the commentary box, a matter-of fact Bill Lawry: 'It's a funny game this cricket, but you'd have to think Queensland only have to bat reasonably well to win it.' True, but first you'd better get the opinion of the fire breather with the ball in his hand.

Bruce Yardley was fielding at mid-off, an unusual field placing for Lillee at the start of an innings, especially when it was a green track.

> Yardley: Clearly Dennis was looking forward to the challenge … He purposefully marked his run-up point and when I threw the ball to him I said 'Good luck, mate.'

He snarled back at me, 'Luck plays no part.' He was in the zone alright! Then he said, '[Viv] might hit this first one into Trinity College [a school way over the leg-side boundary] but then again I might just take his fucken eyes out!' Phew!

Lillee's captain, Rod Marsh:

All I knew was that he was very determined and definitely pissed off with the situation, us having to defend such a poor total. Clearly he thought he'd do something about it—and by being aggressive he was either going to give us a chance or lose the game very quickly.

Lillee pushed off and proceedings were underway in perhaps the most extraordinary opening over seen in a game at this level. The first ball made a statement. Lillee was really tearing in. And, as usual, that ball carried with it all the venom he could muster. Richards contemplated hooking as it went high down leg side, rearing past the West Indian's head.

No matter how good a batsman is, to feel the wind whistling by your ear without a helmet is a daunting experience, to say the least. Lillee really meant that first one. And the second. He was sending them down in excess of 150 kilometres an hour. Marsh and the slips cordon were camped every bit of 30 metres back. The second thunderbolt made Richards duck for cover. Hit in the head by one of these, it's possible that you could be carried off on a stretcher. A 'soft' bouncer can offer the batsman a free hit, but a 'hard' one is as menacing as anything gets in sports. Bob Simpson: 'There's a test on here. A test of supremacy.'

From the bowler's point of view, the bouncer is a weapon. But it has to be used wisely—it's a real 'effort' ball. You have only a certain amount of fuel in the tank and these deliveries can use up plenty of it. But Lillee was on fire. A man with a mission. And he knew he'd only have a short haul that day, it being a one-dayer—at most 8 overs, but, given the short run chase, most likely less.

So, why not another one at Richards's head?

This was a good one and the West Indian flayed at it, giving the man at fine leg a real heart-starter. And enough to bring Bill Lawry out of his early-innings placidity: 'The question is, will the umpire warn Lillee for bowling too many bouncers?' Simpson, who had played for the parochial West, had this response: 'He'll have to be a brave man in Perth.' Lawry again: 'Can't have any more intimidation of the batsman.'

Perhaps Simpson got it right. Umpire Don Hawks, a gentleman if ever there was one, stayed put. Lillee helped him by taking a wide track back to his mark. As Yardley walked close to return the ball to Lillee, he ventured a look that asked the obvious question—any more?

> Yardley: I remember Dennis saying to me, 'Bugger it, I'm going to bowl another one!' It was like a red rag to a bull. One thing you didn't do with Dennis, even at the best of times those days, was tell him what he couldn't, or shouldn't, do. That was the surest way to get him to do it!

Viv Richards, a renowned hooker of the ball, had received plenty around the head area. And in his experience it was the 'skidding' bouncer—for which his West Indian teammate Andy Roberts was feared—that posed the greatest threat. This day, the wicket having hardened, Lillee's were more of the 'flying' type—slightly easier to manage and get out of the way of, if that's what you want. Still, three in a row of any type … yep,

Richards was on his toes for the fourth ball. Another searing bouncer! The crowd, particularly those at the southern end of the ground who could almost touch Lillee's shirt before he started his long run-up, roared with throaty approval.

From behind the wicket we could see Richards's Adam's apple bobbling; he was chewing gum furiously as he stepped away from the wicket. And in the commentary box Bill Lawry couldn't contain himself. 'Watch the umpire and he's warning Dennis Lillee—quite right.' Umpire Hawks moved towards Lillee, who denied him the required eye contact. Hawks's arm out, Lillee brushing it aside. Lillee's memory is hazy. 'Though I was in a bit of a trance at the time, I do recall Don Hawks approaching me and saying "That's enough, Dennis."'

Meantime, Jones couldn't help noticing the effect this salvo was having on Richards, and recalls Lillee's run-in with the umpire differently. 'I honestly saw the whites of Viv's eyes. He was shitting himself. After the fourth one and the umpire tried to speak to Dennis and tell him that was enough ... I heard Lillee say to him, "I run this fucken game." That's when I started shitting *myself*!'

Dennis Lillee continues:

> When we got out there all I can remember thinking is, we have to get rid of Viv and Greg. My thoughts were categorically that if we just tried to bowl line and length then they would have a better chance of getting a start. They'd be good enough to leave, then pick off the runs. Certainly I had no pre-conceived plan to start my attack against Viv the way it turned out. No plans to bounce the hell out of him. I think I was so fired up that I just got carried away. My thought was, 'It's fast, it's bouncy, Viv loves to hook ... and it's either going to be him or me.'

Why I bowled four in a row at him I don't know to this day. But I have to say that my attitude, which seemed very positive at the time, was, if anything, nothing more than bravado—because I wasn't at all sure in my heart of hearts that I really believed we could win from that position.

Would the fifth be another 'head ball'? Tension was mounting out there towards breaking point—sports theatre at its quintessential best. There was a real mind game at play here. Richards knew Lillee wouldn't necessarily bow to the umpire's approach. Would it be five bouncers in a row? You had to take your hat off to Richards, who had the courage to stand firm and react.

Wayne Clark: I was in the gully and just watching Viv's reaction to each ball. The physical change in him was amazing. Not at any stage was there an indication that he was frightened, just an awareness that he had a real battle on his hands. You know, 'How many more of these am I going to get?' You might have thought, well, this is a seaming wicket, so he'll probably pitch the ball up. No way, Lillee was there to intimidate the batsman. And he did.

All eyes were on Lillee as he stormed back to his mark. Where to from here? Kim Hughes, who was fielding at mid-on, provides the answer:

I remember Dennis saying earlier, 'The only way we're going to get Viv is if it pitches leg and hits off.' I'm thinking, 'Hmmm, that'd be pretty useful!' But Dennis just says, 'Give me the ball.' I lob it to him.

It was a length ball on off stump—you miss, I hit. A lesser player may have been excused for edging towards leg, almost before the ball was released, in a bid to get out of the line of fire. But there was Richards, in there defending the ball.

For the next delivery Lillee took it one step further. Calling something across to Yardley at mid-off. 'Roo says I told him "It's over now." I don't think I would have said that, but maybe I did.' Then he placed the ball in his hand and took off, the crowd at his back screaming for blood. And the rest is history. That fabled sixth delivery carried with it all of the great man's massive heart and will. It careered through Richards's defences and on to his off stump. As the vanquished departed, Lillee made a ceremonial leap over the broken trinity, lightly kicking the stump that was lying back on an angle—a bright red mark on it up near the top. In the space of 6 stunning deliveries Dennis Lillee had gone a long way towards giving WA the chance perhaps it hadn't deserved.

A sort of pandemonium erupted in the commentary box. Bob Simpson: 'And the winner on that occasion is Dennis Lillee!' The ever-effervescent Lawry added excitedly:

> Listen to the crowd. They've gone wild! They think they're in with a chance and [watching the replay] there you are, it's ball versus bat and ball has won out. Viv Richards not equal to the occasion. Beautiful bowling.

Lillee says simply of that exquisite delivery:

> 'I managed to put it in the right spot and it landed on the seam and cut back between bat and pad.'

Hughes: I had a perfect view of it. It pitched around middle stump, moved off the seam and just clipped the top of the off stump. Viv wasn't a great back-and-across player, but he did get in behind it. It straightened him up a little bit and it got through his defences. So, what FOT had said in the dressing room he had done out in the middle. Marvellous!

Richards: When I went out to bat I thought here was a good opportunity ... Those [four] bouncers were pretty vicious, quite intimidating. Then he got through to bowl me two balls later—the sort of stuff Dennis Lillee is made of, a measure of what a great bowler he was.

Jeff Thomson: Now Dennis wasn't renowned for bowling yorkers, but on that wicket the ball that got Viv was almost a yorker, otherwise it would have gone over the stumps. I remember Viv coming back into the dressing room, ready to kill somebody. He knew Dennis had set him up and he felt really bad about letting the boys down. We had to let him calm down. Dennis had stitched him up, alright. That fourth bouncer was a real beauty. [Viv] was absolutely ropable that he'd fallen for it.

Greg Chappell: In the dressing room we had a feeling that the first over could have decided the game.

Allan Edwards and Lawrie Sawle were watching from a downstairs viewing area when Dennis bowled Viv. Aware that guests in the President's Room would still be seated at lunch and most likely missing the action, Allan dashed out, burst into the room and announced in a loud voice, 'Dennis has bowled Viv Richards for a duck!'

Those amazing 6 deliveries were a defining moment for the game.

PRIZED WICKET—Dennis Lillee gives his teammates hope—clean bowling danger man Viv Richards.

Richards: Without a Dennis Lillee, it would always be a win for the team batting second and chasing such a modest total. He was so important for the WA side that day. He was the leader and when he immediately started to make things happen, he sent out a message to his teammates. Nobody wanted to be left behind.

Craig Serjeant: I remember thinking that Dennis was going to be a bit reckless and a bit erratic and they might not have to play at too many. What we needed more than anything was to get them playing at everything. When he bowled bouncer after bouncer at Viv, I thought 'Well, this is humorous, but it's not necessarily doing our cause any good.' Of course, the record proves that he was right, because two balls later he bowled Viv. There was genuine excitement among the team—and the crowd—when that happened. That was the defining moment for us in the field that day.

And there was more to come.

Dennis Lillee was ablaze. And he knew his job was not yet done. As he stared down the runway at the new batsman, David Ogilvie, he was all too aware that Greg Chappell was padding up in the Queensland dressing room with WA's paltry total still throbbing down from the scoreboard away to his right.

Ogilvie was one cricketer who would stand out in a crowd—flaming red hair and a bushy beard. In the 1977–78 season he stood out for a different reason—a stellar summer with the bat, producing 1060 runs at 66.25 with six centuries. Form well and truly worthy of a slot in the Australian side, when he made five Test appearances before being dropped for want of form. A correct batsman, with serious powers of concentration.

He'd need that—and more—right now. As Lillee started his run-up Ogilvie considered what was to come. Would another venomous missile be heading down the pitch, this time to him? Lillee didn't let him down, greeting Ogilvie with one that whistled past the batsman's ears. Bill Lawry was on fire, too—a batsman himself, righteously indignant at such an unchallenged full-frontal attack. 'Another bouncer! That's five in the over. Another warning from the umpire.' Then the eight-ball over was finished. What a start to the innings. Those who had witnessed it would never forget it.

Alan Jones, at the non-striker's end:

> When Dennis got Viv out, he turned to me and said, 'What are you looking at?' Well, I'd known him socially, as a mate, but I quickly learned that stuff doesn't necessarily go onto the field. I thought I'd better not show him how I was feeling, so I said, 'You bounce me and I'll put you over the top.' I didn't want to bow my head to him. I knew I was going to cop it anyway.

> Geoff Dymock: We knew that Dennis was fired up. That's the way he played, anyway. He bowled nine bouncers in his first 2 overs and there was a question as to why the umpires didn't move to stem the flow. Nine bouncers in the first 2 overs and ending up a couple of metres from the batsman in the follow-through. Imposing his will on the batsman.

Perhaps working on the theory that simply trying to stay in against Lillee in that mood—with the conditions so favourable—was a high-risk approach, Jones decided to go on the offensive. 'This was my first game back in the side since 1974. I'd just made a couple of centuries in club cricket. I always said if I went back I'd play my natural game.'

Jones took his chances with Lillee's opening partner, Wayne Clark. With the last ball of the second over he swung into action, dobbing Clark back over his head for four. Then took Clark for another boundary in his second over. Jones was beginning to look like he was capable of carrying Queensland close to the victory target, and then he was handed a healthy slice of luck. In Lillee's third over he took a wild swing and skied the ball high to backward point. Craig Serjeant and Bruce Yardley converged.

Serjeant: Roo was at this time in the gully and I was at third slip. We both ran back for the ball and to this day I think it was more my catch than his, but I think I lacked the standing in the team at that stage to get Roo out of the way and the chance went begging.

Yardley: From baseball days I screamed 'mine' and went for it, but I didn't even get a hand on it. A missed chance? Don't know, but I'll never forget Ric Charlesworth, who was fielding nearby at the time, coming up to me, putting his hand on my shoulder and saying, 'Roo, points for having the guts to call it.' Anyway, after that I was banished to third man. I can imagine Dennis screaming 'Get him out of there!' But I'm down there on my own, wondering if I was going to get a bowl.

Serjeant: With so few runs to play with, we had to take every half chance and so when that went down a little wind went out of our sails. Jones was 'in' and as such the most likely player to make the score needed to get his team over the line.

Two balls later—after Jones and Ogilvie had taken the total to 23—Lillee managed to put a stop to proceedings. He induced an edge from Ogilvie that carried low to second slip, where Mick Malone completed an excellent catch, diving forward. The Queenslander had been out there for 19 minutes and faced 13 deliveries for his 9 runs. Importantly, he and Jones had put on 23—just short of a third of the victory target. Lawry was getting into the spirit of things. 'Two for 23 and the crowd's gone wild. Even the TV men are clapping. I've never seen it at a ground.'

For WA the door was now ajar, if only ever so slightly.

Yardley: After Ogilvie went, Bacchus got us in a group and indicated he believed that we could now do it. I'm thinking, 'Can we?'

Mick Malone: I had a feeling that if anybody could do this it was FOT. Plus, we were a confident unit, sort of never beaten.

Bruce Laird: Dennis was bowling like he did before he hurt his back. Tearing in, arms and legs all over the place and hitting the crease fast and hard.

It certainly was a magnificent sight, but with Greg Chappell striding out—and the victory target only 55 runs away—it was still well and truly Queensland's game for the taking. As for the Maroons and Australian captain, it was business as usual.

SAFE HANDS—Mick Malone makes a magnificent diving catch to dismiss David Ogilvie off Dennis Lillee.

Chappell: Getting ready to go out I was in my zone. I felt comfortable. I knew it would be a challenge, but I thought if I could help us see Dennis off we'd be a chance. There was no need to hurry, with such a small total to chase.

For the hungry home crowd though, they were not so sure.

Mr Elegance

Greg Chappell

Pressure. What's that? According to the dictionary: 'Exertion of continuous force'. It's a word used commonly in sporting vernacular, and it talks of situations and opponents applying 'force' on an individual or team within the context of a game. Of being the one to take a kick after the final siren to win a game of football, of a goalie faced with thwarting a penalty shot that could win the game for the opposition, of a batsman working to get through a period of bombardment by fast bowlers on a conducive surface.

Outspoken former Australian cricket great Keith Miller poo-pooed the excessive use of the word, when applied to sports. 'Pressure,' scoffed the World War II pilot, 'is a *Messerschmitt* up your arse.' Few Test cricketers of the modern era would *know* just what Miller was talking about, but most of them would have fully understood the meaning of the word 'pressure' in their world and on many a competition day they would have come face to face with it.

For most of his career Greg Chappell seemed the master of pressure. As a premiere batsman he knew all about the business of getting off the mark … of building an innings … of the nervous nineties … of working his way through a bad slump in form … of taking guard when faced with the imposing threat of a West Indies attack consisting of Roberts, Holding, Croft and Garner. So much chin music. A half volley! What's that? A task tough enough on a benign surface, such as the Adelaide Oval, and a daunting one on the Melbourne Cricket Ground strip of the late seventies and early eighties. When one ball might run along the ground—and the next fly off a length at your unprotected face. In such circumstances sometimes the priority comes down to basic survival—just coming out of it in one piece. Yes, Chappell comprehended all of that, in a career spanning from 1966 to 1984.

If you've been there, too, you'll know that the pressure cooker can tend to wear you down. That in the face of its relentless presence you become more vulnerable to making mistakes. When nerves of steel turn to putty. When, if you're not careful, you can easily start thinking of other places you'd rather be. In the days when Chappell carried the extra burden of captaining the Australian side—on top of being its number one batsman, handy change bowler and gun fieldsman—there was a multiplier factor at work.

On 1 February 1981, Chappell proved that he was mortal like the rest of us and finally succumbed to that eternal enemy— pressure. In a one-dayer against New Zealand at the MCG he made a captain's decision that he would regret for the rest of his days. And it was pitifully sad to witness, as I did from the ABC expert commentator's seat high in the Members' Stand.

At the fall of New Zealand's eighth wicket I saw Greg Chappell slump to the ground where he was fielding at deep mid-off. Seated on his buttocks, arms on his knees acting as a headrest. As Brian McKechnie walked out, needing to hit the final ball of the innings for six to force a draw, Chappell slowly rose to his feet and walked to brother Trevor, who faced the pressure of having to send down the final delivery. 'How's your underarm bowling?' asked Greg. When Trevor responded that he 'didn't know', Greg said, 'Well, you're about to find out.' Umpires and batsman duly advised, Trevor rolled the ball down the wicket.

Greg doesn't try to defend his decision; just to explain it. After a relentless season of cricket, with little respite between games, he and his team were exhausted. Any result other than a win for Australia would mean yet another game in the coming days to take out the series. 'I knew it wouldn't be accepted too well, but at that stage I couldn't have cared less. I just wanted to get off the ground and not have to worry about having to play the extra game.' Of course, the repercussions of that decision will never go away. 'Now I'm going to have to live with it for the rest of my life. Every time cricket's talked about and I'm around, it's going to be brought up by somebody.'

Gregory Stephen Chappell was born on 7 August 1948. In an athletic sense, he was blessed in having two sports-hungry brothers—the older Ian and the younger Trevor—and cricket coursed freely through their family veins. Their maternal grandfather, Vic Richardson, had played for Australia and their father, Martin, was an outstanding Adelaide club cricketer—a good opening batsman, who was known as a fiercely competitive player. In 1950–51 Martin topped the district averages with 513 runs at 42.75. Given all of that, the brothers were bound to take a liking to the grand summer game. And likely to be very good at it. Their mother, Jeanne, would say of them, 'They could keep a straight bat before they could read.' So much did they love the game that they even went to the trouble of importing some wicket soil from a local club ground and, with some assistance, laying a rudimentary pitch running alongside their house in the Adelaide suburbs. They used a tennis court roller to keep it as flat as possible and it was the scene of countless hours of practice and simulated match play.

Though Martin Chappell was quite capable of doing it himself, he wisely anointed another to be his sons' coach. Lynn Fuller, a good former country player who lived nearby and was curator at the local cricket club, set out to teach the lads the fundaments of defensive straight-bat play. Dad rounded off their regular training sessions with robust encouragement in the development of a full array of attacking strokes. A veritable bowling machine, he threw down ball after ball so they could first learn, then rehearse, the techniques that had been drummed into them. He even worked out that a ridge at the front edge of the make-do turf wicket could be used to get the ball to rise sharply and thus teach them how to handle deliveries that threaten the head. Plus, of course, learn how to play the hook shot. Martin Chappell also spent countless hours helping his sons develop their skills in catching, fielding and throwing. A father's priceless contribution. And their bowling skills developed naturally through all those backyard 'net' sessions.

Martin forgave his enthusiastic sons for myriad broken windows in the house, along the way learning the glazier's trade, in replacing one after another, and developing fine diplomatic skills as the neighbours endured cricket balls crashing through their kitchen window. Age was king among the three brothers. Number one dished it out to number two, who in turn lorded it over number three. Painful experiences would be inflicted down the line. One day, number three had had enough. During a bitter argument over a dismissal he stormed off inside the house, returned with a tomahawk, and chased his brother (in this instance, Greg) around the yard until he had to jump a side gate to escape. For Greg, as it was for his brothers, it was all part of a process of toughening up, of taking strides along the path towards becoming a champion cricketer.

If you were to write a script for the nurturing of boys who would go on to the top of the cricket tree, both as players and leaders, you couldn't do better than describe the ascent of the Chappell brothers. Born with the right pedigree, fed and trained right, and given all the encouragement and opportunity they could have wished for, it was no surprise that prodigious talent was evident in all three of them as they grew up. At the age of twelve, Greg hit his first centuries and was selected for the South Australian State schools team. However, he was short for his age and his scoring strokes in those days tended to be mainly to the on-side. In the summer of 1964–65, he had a growth spurt, adding 10 centimetres in seven weeks. Within a year he had shot up to 189 centimetres. With this greater physical presence, Chappell was able to dominate schoolboy matches.

Brother Ian had made his way into the Australian side by the time Greg, at the age of eighteen, was picked to make his state-team debut, against Victoria in the opening game of the 1966–67 season. Scores of 53 and 62 not out. Five games later a promising beginning became even better when he posted his first century for the state, against Queensland in Brisbane. Greg Chappell finished that first season with a commendable 501 runs at 35.78. It was during his second season for the state that he picked up a pearl of wisdom from the legendary Sir Donald Bradman, a regular visitor to the South Australian dressing room before play in home games. As bright as his future was looking at that stage, Chappell was still predominantly an on-side player. And this fact clearly bothered Sir Donald. He took Chappell to one side in the dressing room and said, 'I'd change my grip if I were you.' Greg asked what he meant. 'Well, you'll never be an off-side player with a top-hand grip like that.' Bradman then showed the young Chappell his own grip, with the top hand placement more around to the back of the handle. That was enough for young Greg. He went straight to the nets and—as if by the waving of a magician's wand—opened up the off-side for his attacking strokes.

At the end of the 1967–68 season he took off to play County cricket with Somerset. The opportunity came after WA's John Inverarity withdrew from an arrangement with the County when he was chosen for the Australian tour to England that year. For Chappell it turned out to be a very good learning curve. 'Just playing under different conditions against very good players who were good at using those conditions to their advantage had to make you a better player.' He played for the County the following season and it was during his time there that he continued to develop new skills as a medium-pace bowler. The main benefit, though, was his growing ability to bat in English conditions, which would stand him in good stead in his career later on.

Back home in the 1969–70 season, Chappell dominated with 856 runs at 65.84. Unfortunately though, it wasn't enough to earn him selection on the Australian tour to India and South Africa.

> My name had been mentioned for the 1968 tour to England. I wasn't expecting anything then, but when it came to India and South Africa everybody was talking about me and I had higher expectations. I felt I'd been a bit stiff to miss out, but as it turned out I probably wasn't. I wouldn't have played in India and may have got an opportunity in South Africa, but in pretty ordinary circumstances. It was my luck that I finally got the chance against England the following summer [1970–71]. I'd played against all their bowlers when I was with Somerset.

Instead of India and South Africa, he went to New Zealand with the Australian second team. Then he was named in the 12 for the First Test against England at the Gabba, joining his older brother. It was inevitable that comparisons would be made between the two, and Greg was keen to put them to rest at the time.

> I'm not another Ian Chappell. Ian is shorter and stouter. I'm taller and thinner and I've got more reach. Our range of strokes is completely different. But we are both aggressive and we both like to win.

Greg was named twelfth man for that Test but, after what had seemed to him like a long wait, finally made his debut in the Second, at the WACA Ground in Perth. Slotted to bat at number seven, he walked out, upright as ever but with nerves jangling, of course, to join the tough campaigner Ian Redpath.

Thirty or so twitchy minutes later he scored his first runs and from there the innings blossomed. He went on to post a century on debut, the sixth Australian to achieve the feat, and figured in a stand worth 219 with Redpath. Once he settled in, Chappell played an innings of rare quality. Standing out in the memory are the drives down the ground, mainly off the front foot, but with the occasional gem off the back foot through the off-side. It happened to be the first Test ever played on the WACA Ground—and it will always be remembered as 'Greg Chappell's Game'.

That innings marked down the name of 'Greg Chappell', not only into the record books but also as a batsman to be feared, even revered, by opposition teams for thirteen remarkable seasons to come. When he was in form and in the mood he possessed all the weapons in the armoury of the great—a straight bat, a wide array of strokes, apparent time in which to play those strokes, balance, poise and timing in playing them, plus a desire to make a positive mark on the game.

His own confidence in his ability to be a match changer, and adapt to the circumstances of the game and the playing conditions of the day, made him an invaluable Test player. The hallmark of his game was the flawless correctness of his technique. He possessed the full range of off-side drives, but for absolute elegance and electrifying appeal you couldn't go past his straight strokes on the on-side—back foot and front foot, two of the most difficult strokes in the business, and played by Chappell with consummate ease. Absolutely exquisite! As was the thump through leg when the ball came in short on his left hip. His mastery of placement through the field was of the highest standard. For the purist—and for most others, even the hordes of bowlers who found it so hard to prise him out—Chappell in full flow was a joy to behold.

When Greg Chappell was on song, there was simply no line or length to contain him. One day in Brisbane, WA set a plan for him. Our bowlers tried to maintain a consistent line wide of the off stump, 15 to 25 centimetres down what we used to call 'the corridor of uncertainty', in an attempt to both contain him and, perhaps, tempt him to come at us and to play away from his body. Literally asking him if he'd like to take a risk. Chappell immediately saw what we were up to. His ironclad concentration enabled him to consistently leave the ball alone. Come to me and I'll think about it! Inevitably one of our bowlers strayed in close to off stump, then watched the ball scream away straight down the ground for four. As Chappell touched his bat at the non-striker's end, he whispered in the bowler's ear, 'Why don't you put a few more there?' Game over. We were bored with this tactic long before he was.

On top of the physical genius was almost unbelievable mental toughness, and a commitment to getting on top of the bowling and grinding it into the turf. And then going on to make a big innings. A Greg Chappell virtuoso was like a piano concerto well played. And, of course, he was held in the highest esteem by those around him.

Rod Marsh: You had to get him early but it didn't happen too often. You'd look up to the scoreboard and all of a sudden he'd be 15 or 20—and you'd think, 'We've got trouble here ... how are we going to get him out?'

Jeff Thomson: I never saw Sobers, but I've seen all the best since then—the Pontings, the Laras, the

Tendulkars—and I place Greg Chappell, as far as consistency and the bowling he had to face, as the best at it. All these guys who've been getting runs in recent years, I'd like to see how they'd have gone in the days when Greg was carving out his career. Because these guys today bowl rat-power.

Dennis Lillee: A great batsman. Very determined and very focused. If he got his back up, it seemed he would fight that bit harder. Elegant, competent … had everything. Probably only a notch behind what I saw with Barry Richards and Viv Richards.

John Maclean: He was as tough as any player I've ever seen, with an ability to establish a mental dominance over a bowler for future games.

You would have been forgiven for predicting that it would have been a case of onwards and upwards for Greg Chappell after that magnificent debut innings in Perth. However, there would be a testing time ahead. Chappell admits he perhaps got a bit ahead of himself. He started making poor shot selections and getting himself out. Minor performances with the bat followed for the remainder of the England series and through to the start of the 1971–72 internationals against the 'Rest of the World' side. This caused Chappell to stop and think. He realised the troubles were mental ones.

That's when I started to work on a system of pre-game build-up, a similar pre-innings build-up and extra concentration during each innings. Never making my mind up before a ball was bowled what I was going to do with it. Once you get to Test level your degree of success relates to about 20 per cent physical skills and 80 per cent mental application.

It also encouraged him to develop an early-innings technique of looking to play into 'the vee'—the arc between mid-off and mid-on—until he felt he was settled. With these tweaks, he had turned the corner. His Test batting average soared into the fifties and largely remained there.

Back on English soil for the 1972 tour, Chappell hit the high spots. He topped the tour first-class averages with 1260 runs at 70.00 and, in the five Tests, scored 437 runs at 48.55, with centuries at Lord's and The Oval. From a technical and concentration viewpoint, not to mention the prevailing conditions, Chappell rates the Lord's innings as his best. So does a very good judge, indeed, in Richie Benaud.

> I thought it close to the most flawless innings I had seen and I still believe that to be the case. It was beautifully elegant, with wonderfully executed strokes, great technique and it exhibited a deep knowledge of what was needed to square the series.

To make his performance even more impressive, this marvellous innings had been made during a bowlers' Test, when Australia's Bob Massie claimed a total of 16 wickets on debut. Chappell was able to master the English conditions and dominate the home-side bowlers, drawing deeply on his experience with Somerset.

A successful tour to the West Indies in 1973 followed and he came home to an offer to up sticks and move to Queensland.

Chappell says his first reaction to the Queensland officials' offer was to decline, but in the end he agreed to a one-year term on the understanding that he would be given the captaincy. He saw it as his only way to find an opening against his brother to lead South Australia in the short term.

Queensland agreed to his terms and the incumbent, John Maclean, stood down. The result brought about immediate improvement for Queensland. Greg Chappell, captain for the first time, wearing different colours, narrowly missed a maiden success in the Sheffield Shield competition after losing to NSW in the final at the SCG.

It was a great season for Queensland, and for Chappell it was an exciting time. He had a young and talented group—Martin Kent, Trevor Hohns, Malcolm Francke, Geoff Dymock, Tony Dell, Phil Carlson and Alan Jones—that was topped off when Jeff Thomson agreed to come north. Chappell happily decided to stay beyond his initial one-year term and success finally came Queensland's way in 1975–76, defeating WA for the Gillette Cup in a tense final at the Gabba. This momentum was sufficient to attract Viv Richards, then a rising champion, to join up for the following summer.

> Richards: I liked his captaincy. He was serious and he set the standard for hard work, which I found so important to achieving your goals. He also had a strong commitment to the team and the way he would set goals for the team and for himself.

The success of Chappell's move to Queensland was replicated with some brilliant form in his international career. That first summer (1973–74) produced a run fest, with a massive total of 1880 runs. One particular highlight that season was the

First Test against New Zealand at Wellington where he scored a double century and a century (the fourth batsman in history to achieve this double). And to add to the Chappell family story, brother Ian also scored a century in each innings.

Greg often suffered poor health at this time, traced to problems with his tonsils, which initially doctors were reluctant to remove. During matches he would confine himself to playing hours, plus eating and sleeping. Despite this, though, he was able to glean 608 runs at 55.27 in the six-Test 1974–75 series against England. The following tour to England in 1975, however, was a rare period of sustained failure for Greg, and in four Tests his figures were a total of 106 runs at 21.20.

At the end of that tour to England, brother Ian announced that he'd finished as Australian captain. Greg was the logical replacement skipper, though there was a Victorian-led lobby for Ian Redpath to be given serious consideration. In the end it was a no-brainer. Redpath was 34 and, though an inspirational figure with bat in hand, he was more of a quiet man within the group. Greg Chappell was the new Australian skipper! It was the first time brothers had been accorded the honour. Pre-ordained? Maybe, but you can only imagine the extra stress in having to follow immediately in the footsteps of a brother who had done so well and earned such a high reputation as a leader:

> I had no problem whatsoever in playing under my brother as captain. In fact, I was grateful to have had the opportunity. Sure, it wasn't easy to follow him because he was such a good captain and had such tremendous

rapport with his players ... I came to realise, still do, just how much of an honour and thrill it is to be captain of the Australian cricket team.

Chappell's first challenge as Australian captain was a home series against the West Indies in 1975–76. Which he rose to, as a dream debut as captain unfolded. Ever a man for a big moment, Chappell celebrated his elevation to the captaincy with a century in each innings (123 and 109 not out)—a unique first-up performance in Tests. Australia won the first game by 8 wickets, and went on to win the series 5–1. In the six Tests he scored 702 runs at the Bradmanian average of 117.00—statistics indicating that Chappell relished the added responsibilities of leadership. He would go on to average 55.38 for the 4209 runs he scored in the 48 Tests he captained. That's better than his career average!

The winds of change started blowing the following summer. Pakistan toured (and the series was drawn), Australia ducked down to New Zealand, and then England rode in for the Centenary Test at the MCG. During all of this, player negotiations were under way for World Series Cricket. It was a fraught time. As Australia's captain, Greg Chappell was a prime target. He signed. And really felt the heat when, in England for the 1977 tour, the bubble burst and the cricket world learnt of the imminent mass exodus of players to a new, private organisation.

With the secret signing of so many players to WSC, a dark cloud hung over the England tour. It was a disaster for the Australians, losing the five-Test series three–nil and the three ODIs, two–one. However, WSC itself was by no means a disaster for Chappell. In fact, in the fourteen Supertests they both played, he narrowly eclipsed the great Viv Richards for runs scored—Chappell, 1415 runs, with five centuries at 56.60 ... Richards 1281, with four centuries at 55.59. Adding to the hard numbers, Chappell arguably faced a better quality of bowling from the West Indies and the World XI than Richards did against the full Australian bowling line-up. In the five Supertests in the Caribbean in 1979 he hit a rich vein of form, with 631 runs at 63.10.

Chappell looks back on the WSC experience fondly.

> It was a highlight of my career. I was lucky to have been a part of it. But it was some of the hardest cricket I ever played. One thing I learnt was, making 100 is not enough. As a result, a lot of my really big scores came from the years after WSC.

When the curtain finally came down on WSC, Chappell returned to the Australian captaincy and a role much more complex and demanding than the one he had left. 'It got to the point where I had to shut myself off from the telephone.' He faced up to a tough twin series against England and the West Indies. And proved his mettle—a total of 587 runs from the six Tests at 58.70. Then it was off to England for the Centenary Test at Lord's. Along with teammates Rod Marsh and Dennis Lillee, and England's Chris Old, he was the only player to appear in both celebratory events. And the only man to captain in both games. The fickle London weather ruined the celebration. But a personal total of 106 runs for the game added up to 1074 runs in ten Tests from December 1979 to September 1980.

But the pressure was mounting. And it came to a head in the 1980–81 season with the infamous 'Underarm Incident'— polarising the cricket world and drawing condemnation from the prime ministers on both sides of the ditch. Chappell made himself unavailable for the 1981 tour to England—for 'family and business reasons'. 'I was sure that if I had gone to England it would have been the end of my career.' That decision paved the way for his deputy, Kim Hughes, to lead Australia on what turned out to be a fraught and unhappy mission. Chappell had no expectations about regaining the captaincy, but was 'honoured when the Board chose to give it back to me after 1981'.

The bookends of the 1981–82 season were memorable for Chappell, but the middle was forgettable for the elegant stroke maker. There were split tours with the West Indies and Pakistan and a late-summer trip to New Zealand. In the Second Test against Pakistan in Brisbane he posted his fourth Test double-century. Beyond that, in three Tests (one against Pakistan and two against the West Indies) and five World Series Cup one-day internationals, he made just 82 runs in eleven innings. Almost unbelievably for a player of his class, in that period he'd been dismissed without scoring five times and reached double figures only three times. But, typical of Chappell, through it all he never lost his sense of humour. When it was suggested that he might be out of form, his reply was that he 'hadn't been out there long enough to find out!' As humiliating as it was, Chappell considered the slump a good experience for him. 'It made me a better cricketer and a better person. The worst part of it lasted only three weeks or so, but it felt like three years!'

The horror stretch came to an end in New Zealand when he made a century in the first ODI. Then he cemented a return to form with 176 in the Third Test at Christchurch, an innings described as one of the greatest and most effortless in modern-day Test cricket. Looking back on that time, Chappell says:

Basically the fault was mental. I was unable to get my normal mental preparation working before the Test matches. I was mentally unfit and the more I tried to force it the harder things got. I was walking in to bat knowing my outlook was wrong. It was as if I felt I was going to fail.

Again, Chappell stood down from a tour, this time against Pakistan before the start of the 1982–83 home season. Again he was reinstated as skipper for the coming tour by England. The challenge for him and the team was to regain the Ashes. He achieved that goal and in the five Tests scored 389 runs at 48.62, with centuries in Perth and Adelaide. The latter completed a full hand—a century in each of the Australian states at that time hosting Test matches. At series end he quit the captaincy for the final time. Though he was called up for a brief tour of Sri Lanka, when Kim Hughes was unavailable.

As it turned out, the master batsman would play only one more season for Australia—and end it on an amazing high. Pakistan toured. He made an unbeaten 150 in the Second Test at Brisbane, but it was the Fifth Test at Sydney that left the happiest memories. Going into the game he had things on his mind—it would be his last Test, he needed 69 runs to surpass Sir Donald Bradman's record for the most runs scored by an Australian in Tests (6996), and two catches to go past Colin Cowdrey's world Test catching record (120). All were achieved. Kim Hughes did the right thing, elevating him from number six to his old spot at four, and a great player ended a great career with a great innings. Chappell rates this 182 as mentally the best innings he ever played. And it meant he became the first batsman in Tests to post a century in both his first and last innings. It was all over. He summarised his career like this: 'I was lucky to have had natural talent, but the main reason for my success was concentration.' Rod Marsh and Dennis Lillee also retired in that game. It was the end of an era.

They say records are made to be broken, and Greg Chappell left them strewn all over the place when he retired. Let's begin with his overall Test and WSC Supertest record: 101 games, 8525 runs, twenty-nine centuries, average 54.29. In the 48 Tests which he captained, Chappell averaged 55.38; in the 39 Tests when he wasn't captain, he averaged less than 52. His total of 380 runs off his own bat in a Test in New Zealand stood as a world record. His performance in taking seven catches in the Perth Test against England in 1974–75 still stands as the world record (shared with India's Yajurvindra Singh, Sri Lanka's Hashan Tillakaratne, New Zealand's Stephen Fleming and Australia's Matthew Hayden). Chappell also adapted successfully to limited-overs cricket. He played in only 74 ODIs, but at retirement his tally of 2331 runs was a record for the format. His average (40.18) and strike rate (75.70) were very good for the time (although not so fancy in this day and age).

And Chappell was no slouch with the ball. His medium-pacers, released from a high position, were hard to handle when conditions were even slightly favourable to his style, with movement through the air and off the wicket. It could be said that, as a captain, he tended to under-bowl himself. When once asked about this, a typical Chappell reply: 'Oh, other guys are picked to do that job, so I let them.' In Tests he claimed 47 wickets at 40.70. Handy. But in ODIs he bagged 72 at 29.12, including a match-winning haul of 5–15 against India in Sydney in 1981. Add to that his marvellous fielding and catching skills and you

have something approaching an all-rounder. Some of his fielding skills were inherited from his grandfather, some developed
during the practice routines Martin put the boys through. Part
of the secret lay in his attitude. 'I loved fielding. It's a challenge.
It's you against the batsman.' And on out-fielding: 'When you're
batting you try to penetrate the field. With fielding it's the opposite view. You must read into the batsman, how he plays and what
he's thinking.'

Captains of the Australian cricket team rarely find themselves on the scrap heap after they have retired as a player—their
input to the game, in one form or another, is far too important to
be overlooked. Greg Chappell is no exception in this. Over the
30 years since his retirement as a player he has made contribu-
tions in a number of ways, and in a number of countries. Still
does, in fact, as Cricket Australia's National Talent Manager. But
to trace the story since 1984, soon after he finished as a player
he was drafted into the role of national selector. At the same
time he also became a member of the Australian Cricket Board
(now Cricket Australia). He resigned from both roles in 1988,
but returned for a short stint as a selector in 2010–11. Chappell
was for five seasons (from 1998–2003) coach of his native
state, South Australia. He has also worked as a consultant at
Pakistan's National Cricket Academy (2004), and occasionally
taken the microphone as a commentator for ABC radio. He was
inducted into the Sport Australia Hall of Fame in 1986, and in
2002 was inducted into the Australian Cricket Hall of Fame.

Chappell's highest-profile appointment came in 2005, when
he accepted a two-year contract to coach the Indian national
team leading up to the 2007 World Cup. Given India's growing
status in world cricket, the spotlight was bound to fall fairly
and squarely upon the Australian. During that time there was
a mixture of achievement and controversy. The controversy

was the result of Chappell's relationship with Sourav Ganguly, who was captain at the time of his arrival. Ganguly alleged that Chappell asked him to stand down as captain, and the Indian media got behind their captain. Ganguly was later dropped by the selectors, for lack of form, but rumours abounded that his dismissal was as a result of his relationship with the coach.

During his tenure as coach, though, there were some very positive results. India won its first Test series in the West Indies since the 1970s (without batting the great Sachin Tendulkar) and won its first-ever Test match in South Africa. In one-day internationals, India broke Australia's world record of seventeen consecutive wins chasing down targets. India performed poorly at the 2007 World Cup, winning only one game and failing to reach the 'super eight' stage. Yet Chappell was offered a further contract. Which he declined.

Life goes on for Greg Chappell. Enjoying his involvement with the nation's best young cricketers. Time with wife Judy and their children and grandchildren. Playing golf, which he does admirably. And just kicking back.

The gloveman

Rod Marsh

So you want to be a wicketkeeper when you grow up? Well, consider this—just as much as the need for sharp reflexes, nimble feet and sure hands, you're going to need a big slice of luck. Because usually there's only one 'keeper in every side. And if somebody has beaten you to it, you could have a devil of a time getting rid of that somebody and taking over. Just ask Barry Jarman. When Gil Langley retired from the Australian post in 1957, Jarman was widely tipped to take over. But the selectors went for the 30-year-old Wally Grout. He proved to be one of our very best and Jarman had to spend a long time as his understudy. In the end he cobbled together just nineteen Test appearances, often only getting a game when Grout was injured. Pop the same question to Bob Taylor. When the England selectors called 'time' on John Murray in 1967, Taylor, at twenty-six, was seen as the logical replacement. But along came the twenty-one-year-old Alan Knott, and Taylor, one of the prettiest glovemen you could ever wish to see, had to settle for the role of bridesmaid. For a long time. Indeed, his first England cap was a charity job in New Zealand (1970–71), when Ray Illingworth decided to reward Taylor for his patience and 'rested' Knott to give the perennial tourist a Test cap.

Rod Marsh faced the same dilemma. In his home state of WA he ran up against a fellow called Gordon Becker, first at club level, forcing Marsh to make his debut for West Perth's first team as a batsman. Frustrated at his lack of wicketkeeping opportunity, Marsh booked a course at the University of Western Australia, just to have a nailed-down go behind the stumps with the students' team. But it wasn't long before Becker again stood in his way—this time for the 'keeper's job in the state team.

The main problem for the young contender was that, as well as being a solid wicketkeeper, Becker was also more than handy with the bat. Marsh, though, could also bat, and eventually found his way into the WA side, against the West Indies in 1968—as the number five batsman, two slots ahead of Becker, who had the gloves. Marsh knew he had to earn his keep with the bat if he was ever to get an opportunity as a wicketkeeper. In a game that included the great West Indian pace duo of Wes Hall and Charlie Griffith (admittedly, in the twilight of their careers), Marsh had a challenge on his hands. And when he was bowled by Griffith for a duck in the first innings, things weren't looking too good.

In the second innings he was dropped before he had scored. At 30 another chance, but after that the nerves settled and Marsh went on to post a century. That earned him a place in the Combined XI (the WA team bolstered by Ian Chappell, Doug Walters and Paul Sheahan) to play the West Indies the following week. Batting at number four in that august company, he went without scoring in the first innings—prompting the impish comment, 'It really isn't such a bad game. I mean 0, 104, 0 … the way things are going I'll get a century in the second innings and I'll end up averaging 50 for my career.' Actually, Marsh made 22 in the second innings and was retained as a batsman for five Sheffield Shield games, before a lack of runs cost him his place. Imagine, then, his joy when, shortly before the first WA team was announced the following season, Becker retired. And so a wondrous career as a wicketkeeper-batsman was launched. At no stage did Marsh look back—through to his retirement in 1984. But it wasn't always an easy path to tread.

The 1969–70 season, his first as permanent 'keeper, was a time of quality consolidation for Marsh. In eight games for the state he returned 31 dismissals—eight of them stumpings. And he batted with authority to score 473 runs at 39.40, falling one run short of a maiden Sheffield Shield century, against NSW in Perth. All of which added up to selection for the First Test against England the following season, and when Marsh would take his first steps down a tricky path.

The previous summer Australia had toured South Africa, with Brian Taber (NSW) the main custodian and Ray Jordon (Victoria) his deputy. And John Maclean (Queensland) had been preferred to Marsh for a second-team tour to New Zealand. So, when Marsh was chosen ahead of that trio for the First Test, the wolves started baying. What didn't help matters was the fact that in his debut game, in Brisbane, Marsh turfed three chances. When he then dropped Geoff Boycott in Perth there was a serious cry for him to be replaced. During the series a writer dubbed him 'Iron Gloves'. (He already had a nickname within the WA side. The previous season we had travelled by train from Melbourne to Adelaide and when it pulled up at a country town one of us looked out the window and there it was—'Bacchus Marsh'. That's you, mate!)

The harassment Marsh suffered wouldn't go away. Particularly in Brian Taber's home town of Sydney. When Marsh played at the SCG in 1971–72 in an international against the 'Rest of the World' the crowd gave him a real pasting. When he came out to bat it was as if the Hill mob were barracking for the opposition! So pointed was the hostility that even the jilted Taber, one of nature's true gentlemen, felt obliged to pat Marsh on the back and wish him all the best. And in the dressing room at the end of play one day Taber actually apologised to Marsh for the crowd's behaviour.

The game, though, was to prove a turning point for Marsh. With Australia struggling at 5–163 he came to the crease to join Sydney favourite John Benaud. The pair put on an invaluable 69 and Marsh went on to be unbeaten on 77 when the innings ended. A few red-blooded shots and the lads on the Hill started to applaud him. And they would continue to give him wonderful support through the rest of his illustrious career.

Fate plays strange cards sometimes. In Rod Marsh's case, if his mother had had her way, he might have been a pianist, not a cricketer. While he and elder brother Graham both loved backyard cricket, joined by their father and mates, their mother barely tolerated this activity because of the threat it posed to her beloved garden. The young Marsh also loved to play football, and his mother hated it. Instead she wanted him to learn to play the piano well and was worried that he might damage his hands in the winter game. And that's just what happened.

Marsh broke a tendon in a finger of his left hand … playing football! Piano practice was two hours every day and Marsh knew he was in for the high jump if he was unable to take his seat that day. Possible excuses were adding up to nothing. He badly needed to devise a plan—and leapt at the chance to go out to the front lawn to retrieve the afternoon newspaper. A chance to think of something. Coming back in, he contrived to make it look as though he got the injured finger caught in the door lock. Letting out a loud scream, he raced into the kitchen and shouted, 'I think I've broken my finger!' He was rushed to the local hospital and had the finger set in plaster. Parents none the wiser.

A couple of years later, aged fourteen and a student at Armadale High School, Marsh won a book prize for a poem he entered in a school competition. It read:

> Hither and thither he dives about,
> Wot's 'is name? Wally Grout.
>
> There's a spinner who spins them low,
> Wot's 'is name? Richie Benaud.
>
> He'll chew and chew till he does die,
> Wot's 'is name? Ken Mackay.
>
> From his bat runs do emerge,
> Wot's 'is name? Peter Burge.
>
> He has the English in a frenzy,
> Wot's 'is name? Graham McKenzie.
>
> With his bumper he does haunt,
> Wot's 'is name? Ronnie Gaunt.

There's a bowler who gets the stick,
Wot's 'is name? Ian Quick.

From the covers he shouts an appeal,
Wot's 'is name? Norm O'Neill.

On the English I know I've been harsh,
Wot's me name? Rodney Marsh.

Golf was a very popular topic in the Marsh household. Both Mum and Dad were keen participants, so it followed that the boys would take up the game. Graham represented WA in the Australian schoolboys cricket championships, but his sporting career veered strongly in the direction of golf. He turned professional in 1969 and had 70 wins on the money circuit, also receiving acclamation as a premier golf course designer. Younger brother Rod, a natural left-hand bat, had to play golf right-handed because there were no left-hand clubs in the house. Despite this handicap, he became proficient enough at the game to play more than one sub-par round.

So what made Rod Marsh want to become a wicketkeeper?

The inspiration came from a teacher, who talked him into taking the gloves for the school team when he was ten. It was an immediate love affair. Young Marsh would spend hours throwing a ball against a brick wall and catching it. Like Sir Donald Bradman before him, he would also use a golf ball, which would rebound fast and at unpredictable angles. He'd also throw a cricket ball against the cylindrical upright of the clothes hoist on the back lawn—for diving practice. Along the way he developed a work ethic that would stay with him forever.

As he advanced in first-grade cricket with the university club, Marsh began to eye the top of the tree. The ambition burned within him. Proof lay in a letter he wrote in the winter of 1968 to his club captain, John Inverarity, who was on tour in England with the Australian team. He signed it off, 'By the way, in case you hadn't realised it, this letter is being written by Australia's next Test wicketkeeper'. That promise was fulfilled a little over two years later, though at the time of writing he hadn't even represented his state! It all happened quite quickly. Picked for WA as a batsman in 1968–69, taking over as the state's 'keeper the following season, and capped for his country the summer after that.

It was at the beginning of his second season for WA, against Queensland in Brisbane, that Marsh teamed up for the first time with Dennis Lillee, forming a partnership that would prove to be the best of the best. And, in that game, for the first time these words were written: 'Caught Marsh, Bowled Lillee'. The victim was Keith Dudgeon. It would become an oft-repeated line.

For most sportspeople, that dream moment when you reach out and touch the Holy Grail—in Rod Marsh's case his first selection to represent Australia—means the world. For Marsh, though, it was almost an anticlimax. In Brisbane at the time, with the WA side, he went to bed unaware that the national team had been named that night. At 6.45 the following morning the phone rang in his motel room. It was his wife, Roslyn, screaming down the line, 'Congratulations! They've picked the

Australian team and you're in it.' Marsh pinched himself, woke his roommate, grabbed a bottle of beer from the bar fridge and celebrated with a 7 am toast.

The selection, for the first game of the 1970–71 Ashes series, also took the media by surprise and a number of them went to town, criticising Marsh's inclusion and suggesting he'd be further found out because he'd be unable to 'pick' the mystery deliveries of NSW spinner John Gleeson. Marsh shrugged off the doubts. Having faced Gleeson three weeks before in a Shield game in Sydney, he felt he had it all worked out. Unlike some of his WA teammates, myself included. He was looking on from the other end while I muddled around, clearly unable to tell what was coming at me. At the end of a Gleeson over he came up to me and said, 'You can't pick him, can you?' 'Well, no.' 'Mate, I can tell what he's doing from the way he places the ball in his hand at the top of his run-up. Do you want me to give you a signal?' My response doesn't bear repeating!

Marsh handed his critics the advantage in his first outing in the baggy green cap, dropping those three chances and offering little with the bat. Until, that is, the Fifth Test in Melbourne, when captain Bill Lawry left Marsh high and dry on 92—eight runs short of becoming the first Australian 'keeper to make a Test century. That declaration may have cost Lawry his job. He was replaced by Ian Chappell after the Sixth Test in Adelaide. Coincidentally, that had been Dennis Lillee's first game for his country. And he'd taken 5–84 in the first innings.

The planets were aligning. The 1971–72 tour by the 'Rest of the World' passed quietly for Marsh, but the 1972 visit to England began brilliantly for him. In the opening Test at Old Trafford he made 91 and took five catches in the second innings. In his tenth Test match appearance, the Fourth Test at Leeds, he claimed his first stumping—Alan Knott, off the bowling of Ashley Mallett.

And who will ever forget his joyous rampage after hitting the winning run in the final Test at The Oval? Incidentally, the final day of that game featured the first live telecast of a game into Australia, thanks to satellite technology—and people at home were able to watch on. Australia lost the series, but Marsh got a consolation prize—he'd broken Wally Grout's record for dismissals in a series in England.

If you were to track Marsh's career with the bat, there would be some spikes and some troughs. In 1972, feeling he was a more complete batsman from his experiences on the tour of England, he pushed John Inverarity for a rise to number five in the WA batting order—and promptly embarked on a run spree. It began with a blistering 236 against Pakistan, at the time the highest score by a WA-born player. In that innings he showed a wide array of scoring strokes, most played with the brutal power that was a hallmark of his batting throughout. He believed every ball was a potential boundary. That innings against Pakistan, which remained the highest score in his career, set things going, and over a 42-day period he added three more centuries, scoring 790 runs with the stellar average of 79. Included in those centuries was 118 in the Adelaide Test against the Pakistanis. Now he *had* become the first Australian wicketkeeper to compile a Test century! However, it wasn't a particularly pretty innings in fairly easy conditions, and Marsh rated his two previous scores in the nineties against England as being better knocks.

Through dint of his batting, particularly early in his career, Marsh was a genuine all-rounder at the Test level. Paving the way for those to follow: Ian Healy, Adam Gilchrist and Brad Haddin—all multiple century-makers in Tests. In every sense he broke the mould from which 'keepers were made—which had been first and foremost to be good behind the stumps. If they added a bit of sting to the tail, all well and good, but the primary demand was that they be able to take everything cleanly.

There was to be a third score in the nineties—out for 97 in the First Test against the West Indies in Kingston, Jamaica (1973)—before he posted another three-figure score, this time against New Zealand in Adelaide the following season. Then came a fairly bleak period—only three half-centuries in 39 innings leading up to his second innings in the 1977 Centenary Test at the MCG. Admittedly, during that period he had been part of decisive home series victories over England (1974–75) and the West Indies (1975–76). However, his unbeaten 110 in the Centenary Test included a partnership of which legends are made. Rick McCosker, his jaw broken in the first innings, diced with death to help Marsh add a vital 54 runs.

That was pretty well it for Marsh the batsman. As his bright light flickered and faded—dulled by an almost-incessant West Indies pace barrage—he posted just five more half-centuries in Tests. A once-proud batting average declined to finish at 26.52 when he retired in 1984, with only one other 'major' century—an unbeaten 102 in the second innings of the final WSC Supertest at Antigua in 1979. But there'd been enough big moments for state and country for the burly left-hander's batting to be given a healthy tick.

There's more than a 'well done', though, for his work behind the stumps! Through dint of hard work on fitness and skills development and maintenance, Marsh at his height was as good as the best. His 97 Tests produced a then world-record total of 355 dismissals, but it's worth noting that he was still at the top of his game in 1982–83, a year before retirement. In five home Tests against England he pocketed twenty-eight dismissals, including a career-best nine in the Second Test in Brisbane. His best for WA was eleven in a game. Yes, old Iron Gloves certainly did strut the stuff!

From the get-go Marsh made sure he was always the focal point in the field. His body wasn't built for speed, but he was very fast over a short distance. This helped him get up to the wicket for returns every time, even when he was standing way back to the likes of Jeff Thomson and his mate Lillee. He was a target for the throw in, waving his arms in the air to improve the sight line of a fieldsman with the ball out in the deeps. And his acrobatic work in retrieving a wild throw saved many an overthrow, while making the odd 'impossible' run-out. He was the first I saw to throw the ball to the heavens after taking a catch. Showmanship? Well, yes, but it certainly served to give his teammates a lift. At the start of one season for WA (I think it was 1973–74), he actually stopped the practice and we all wondered what was wrong. In the end John Inverarity, one of cricket's most upright and understated characters, asked him to please pick it up again and give his teammates something to enthuse about. By the same token, I believe Dennis Lillee was the first bowler to cry 'catch' when a hit or snicked ball was in the air. A practice that could be rather disconcerting when standing back 30-odd metres at the WACA Ground with one coming your way in the slips at a hundred miles an hour!

In one way, Marsh was absolutely 'typical'. Wicketkeepers are a bit of a breed, often choosing to sit in the darkest corner of the dressing room and keeping a grubby, fusty-smelling bag. I remember Rod going through a stage of staying with the same shirt for the whole four days of a WA game—if he'd had a good outing (with either gloves or bat) on day one. If that happened during a hot spell, and you were down to stand near him in the slips, you'd try awfully hard to stay upwind of him!

Leadership was another subject. I am not alone in the belief that, given the opportunity, he would have made an indelible mark as Australian captain. Some believe that chance should have come after Ian Chappell retired, and before World Series Cricket in 1977–78. At that time, though, he was busy polishing his act as skipper for WA. I played under him, and in the first season (1975–76) the learning curve was steep. However, the next summer he made a huge impression—leading his team to double success in the Sheffield Shield and Gillette Cup. We had been accustomed to the studious and careful approach of John Inverarity, and then along came the inspirational 'follow me' style of Marsh.

In that second season he was every bit the equal of Inverarity as a leader. I remain convinced that he should have been given the Australian job after the big WSC compromise. Not only would the team have embraced his 'do-as-I-do' brand of leadership, but this would also have left Kim Hughes free, for the time being, to express himself solely with his flashing blade. As it turned out Hughes had the job, albeit on-and-off with Greg Chappell, and, as a result, those post-WSC years were far from contented times in the Australian camp. And on the troubled 1981 tour of England, where Marsh and Dennis Lillee had problems with the way Hughes ran things, even the most disinterested observer could sense that things weren't right.

Having seen at close hand the dimensions of Marsh's leadership qualities—his man-management skills and his grasp of the strategic side of the game—I felt sure that there would be a life after cricket for him … in cricket. First he was snapped up by the media and ended up a television broadcaster. And he was good. But better was to come … for cricket. In 1991 he was appointed head coach of the Australian Cricket Academy in Adelaide, where he did a marvellous job running a finishing school for a generation of Australian players. In 2001 he left the Australian job and took up as inaugural director of the English academy. He held that position for four years, during which time he also acted as an England selector. Beyond that, he helped set up the ICC's Global Cricket Academy in Dubai.

Rod Marsh is nothing if not a character—a man with a sharp sense of humour, a great storyteller and possessor of a ready throaty laugh. In other words, he is very engaging company and at times a real larrikin. These days he's rather partial to a glass of quality red wine, but in his early times as a cricketer it was strictly beer … and more beer.

So, on the way to England for the 1983 World Cup he took up a challenge—to post a record number of cans drunk during the flight between Sydney and London. He managed 45. It is legend that teammates had to carry him out on a luggage trolley. Incidentally, the record didn't last long. In 1989, David Boon waltzed past it, posting a total of 52. Player behaviour is so tightly managed these days that Boon's mark is pretty safe.

Depending on who you are, where you're playing, the state of the game and who's bowling, you might be happy with a dot ball. But a four or a six was always was more in Rod Marsh's style. There are some for whom the thought of clearing the ropes for a 'maximum' never enters the mind, but what if the maximum is more than a six?

Well, at the MCG in the Third Test against New Zealand (1980-81), Marsh was involved in one. To really appreciate this story you have to know that, before the ropes were brought into the game, the MCG boundary, extending to the fence, was a mighty big ground for cricket. It wasn't at all a rarity for batsmen to run a five. On this day the Black Caps openers, Bruce Edgar and John Wright, had done just that. Hared off for an all-run five. But they were cutting it a bit fine and when the ball was returned from the outfield to Marsh he shied at the bowler's end, looking for a run-out. Trouble was, he missed the stumps and the ball careered off to the boundary, the fortunate batsman accorded a 'nine'! Knowing Bacchus, he'd have afforded a wide grin under that moustache and shaken his head.

The following comments attest to how much he was loved and respected, for a wide variety of reasons.

> Viv Richards: I thought playing against him, though he was a bit of a rogue and always a little untidy, that he had it in him to be something special. He has a good cricket brain and was a born leader. I have a tremendous amount of respect for him.

> Rob Langer: His attitude was 'we're here for one thing, and that is to win this game'. A slightly larrikin style, outward going, robust in terms of competitiveness towards the other side and individual players ... and never taking a backward step.

> Greg Chappell: Bacchus was one of only two players I knew who'd kill to play for Australia. The other was Ian Redpath.

Bruce Laird: Just tough. Absolutely loyal. Good cricket brain. Should have been an Australian captain.

Jeff Thomson: He used to wind me up. At the end of my early overs in a Test I'd ask him how he thought I was going. One day he clearly thought I wasn't going too well at all. He beat me to the question, saying 'Well bowled, Cheryl'—and you understand where he was coming from when you know that Cheryl is my wife's name. He was trying to get me going. I said, 'I'll show you, you little wombat!' And went back and tried to hit his gloves as hard as I could.

Bruce Yardley: When I bowled with him behind the stumps I always felt he was with me on all levels. He would prompt me to achieve something and keep me on track. Just little things, like he'd meet you mid-pitch after an over and say, 'Weren't we having a drink the other night and you told me that you'd finally arrived, that you'd learnt to persevere and that you had this new self-belief. Well, I've been waiting here for two overs for a fast ball down leg side and it hasn't come! What the fuck's going on?'

Mick Malone: I played under Ian and Greg Chappell, John Inverarity and Kim Hughes, plus a couple of others around the place, and I have no doubt that Bacchus was the best. He had an understanding of the game, and of his players, and a way about him that I loved. He had the wonderful ability to do something to break the dressing room tension. There was a one-dayer between Australia and the West Indies at the WACA Ground and it was a really lively pitch which the Windies quicks were thoroughly enjoying. Bruce Laird was batting and Joel Garner was pounding them in and they were flying high through to the 'keeper. The Australian group in the dressing room were understandably pretty tense, but I remember Bacchus yelling out, 'I want my mummy!' Everyone just broke up and suddenly much of the tension had vanished.

Ric Charlesworth: I started playing cricket with him when I was twelve and he was fifteen, in the West Perth under-sixteens. He'd open the bowling, put on the pads and keep for a while, take the pads off and bowl some spin, put the pads on again … then open the batting. He was the whole show. He proved to be a very good judge of cricket and cricketers—tactically very astute. But that was fortified by a personality that was positive and reinforcing and supportive. Rod did his guidance and tuition in a subtle way. I got out in the eighties in a game against Pakistan one day. He just drifted past me in the dressing room and said, 'Don't you like making hundreds?'

Who better than Marsh's great partner and friend over time, Dennis Lillee, to sum up an incredible relationship with a marvellous player and personality:

I suppose you could call the relationship between Rod and me over our years with WA and Australia as a mixture of camaraderie, respect and partnership.

As a wicketkeeper he was the most complete. The secret to his success was that his technique was so sound. Combine that with lightning reflexes and he was taking wide balls standing upright and on the inside of his body when others would be sprawling out to make a diving attempt. Plus, he had the ability to pull off that great catch that could turn a match.

You couldn't fail to respect his wonderful competitive spirit. He was always prepared to throw down the gauntlet and stick his chest out and have a go … It saddens me that he wasn't given the chance to show his talents as a leader for Australia. With the bat he certainly was a match-winner when he was on his game. Not a quiet collector of runs, but a player who went out and helped himself to them.

He would come up to me before a session and discuss the batsmen we were likely to see that day—and he'd let me know his thoughts, either criticism or praise, at the end of the day's play. Occasionally, too, if my game was a little bit off there'd be a helpful hint about my technique. His catchcry as captain of WA was 'professionalism'. That one word goes a long way to describing Rod's sustained success. He simply applied himself absolutely to the task and left no stone unturned in his effort to be the best.

As a bowler–wicketkeeper combination, Lillee and Marsh remain the most effective duo the cricketing world has ever seen. A team within a team. Each inspired in the other a will to lift their game, to work together and bring the opposition down.

By the time Lillee and Marsh had both pulled stumps, after the 1983–84 series against Pakistan, 'caught Marsh, bowled Lillee' had appeared 95 times in Test matches. Indeed, of Marsh's career total of 923 dismissals in all Tests, WSC Supertests and other first-class games a phenomenal 238 would be off Lillee's bowling. He gets the nicks, I catch 'em!

To cap off this remarkable partnership on the statistician's board, at the point of their retirement both Lillee and Marsh had claimed 355 dismissals in Tests. An incredible coincidence! For each, that stood at the time as the world record—names side by side again.

A clever plan

The score was 2–23 and, for Lillee and his captain, it was time to up the ante. Australia's greatest batsman of the era was coming to the crease with only 54 runs to chase down. Lillee prepared to execute. From the commentary box, Bill Lawry offered 'Champ to champ again—and the crowd are calling "kill … kill …".'

It was time to draw on that 'team within a team'—Lillee's long-standing and very successful partnership with Rod Marsh. Their unique teamwork on the pitch was a case of one and one makes three—not just wonderful bowling and wicketkeeping skills, but combined 'thinking' as well. So many times the two had worked together to bring about a batsman's downfall, and with a place in the Gillette Cup final at stake, it was time to put this wonderful understanding to work again.

> Marsh: We'd talked on several occasions before about
> Greg being a chance hooking leg side. I put my glove up

and called Dennis to give me one high down leg side. Of course, I then went back to my position behind the stumps. I knew he would bowl it there and before he let it go I was heading off down leg side. Greg went for it and got quite a good piece of it, actually, and was more shocked than anyone when he turned with the shot and saw me just standing there waiting for it.

As easy as that? Not really. For Lillee, it was the not-so-simple matter of getting the ball exactly where his captain had called for it. And Marsh had to trust that his mate would find the right line and not leave him to watch the ball fly over the stumps for four byes.

> Dennis Lillee: It was a masterpiece of strategy by Bacchus. We all knew that Greg was very good at pulling, but he hooked with the flight. I don't know that we got him too often with that tactic, but Bacchus obviously believed that with the bouncy wicket, and the short run chase, Greg would definitely have a go. The second part of it was the execution. Thankfully, I was able to deliver it in the right spot, because before I let the ball go Bacchus had moved to a position well to the leg side of his usual stance. That meant when Greg got a fine edge on it he was there waiting for the catch, rather than cursing as the ball ran away fine of our fine leg for a boundary. He trusted that I could do my bit. It was marvellous stuff by him, great captaincy. That really was the backbreaker.

That Lillee was able to hit the spot in those circumstances is yet another measure of the man's greatness—concentrating on sending one down on a line and length he would never have practised. It was sheer genius. We watched, entranced, as Chappell made to glide the ball to the fine-leg boundary, looking to get it wide of the 'keeper and fine of the man at fine leg, but instead watching it land safely in Marsh's expectant gloves.

Not all the WA players out in the middle had seen the Marsh signal. For some, however, it was enough to sharpen their concentration.

> Rob Langer: I was standing at fine leg and when I saw Rod's call, I was immediately on my toes. 'Ooooh. I'd really better get alert here!' I was already aware how much bounce Dennis was getting, thinking if anyone really goes for one of these it will come down my way very high.

> Kim Hughes: I was at mid-on and what I saw was an endorsement for the theory that great bowlers often come with great wicketkeepers. They are a partnership. When Dennis got to within five or so metres of his delivery leap, which I was aware of out of the corner of my eye, I could see Bacchus move strides to his left. To be able to respond to his mate's call and get the ball in the right spot was freakish, absolutely brilliant.

> Mick Malone: That was just one of the great pieces of captaincy. Not to mention a great piece of bowling.

In a trice it was Queensland 3–27, with Richards and Chappell back in the pavilion, 2 runs between them. Chappell admits he was taken by surprise at the tactic. 'I was unaware of the plan between Dennis and Rod. I generally let the high ones go, but decided to try and help that one on its way—and just gloved it.' But he wasn't going to go that easily. Chappell stood his ground and waited for the umpire's nod.

Alan Jones, camped at the non-striker's end, once again had a front-row view of the theatre that was unfolding:

> I saw Rod indicate he wanted one down leg side. Greg got a touch on it, but didn't want to go. There was a bit of a chorus of 'You blokes are never out.'

> Bruce Yardley: Though we had no doubt, there was a little conjecture about whether Greg had actually hit it. Years later, actually at the twenty-fifth-anniversary reunion of the match, Greg owned up, with a twist. 'I swear to you that I did not hit that delivery (pause) it hit me!'

As umpire Hawks's finger went up it was almost too much for Lawry. '"Long live Dennis Lillee" is the cry at the WACA Ground.' Then, as things settled down a little, 'It is one of the pleasures in cricket, watching a great fast bowler in action— we're seeing that today.' This incredible breakthrough came with the fourth ball of Lillee's fourth over. His figures as Greg Chappell departed: A heady 3–11, with two of the most prized scalps in world cricket among them. Thanks to WA's champion fast bowler, the pendulum had taken a distinct swing in the home team's direction.

The Queensland dressing room looked on in stunned silence as a bemused Chappell headed their way. There had been an

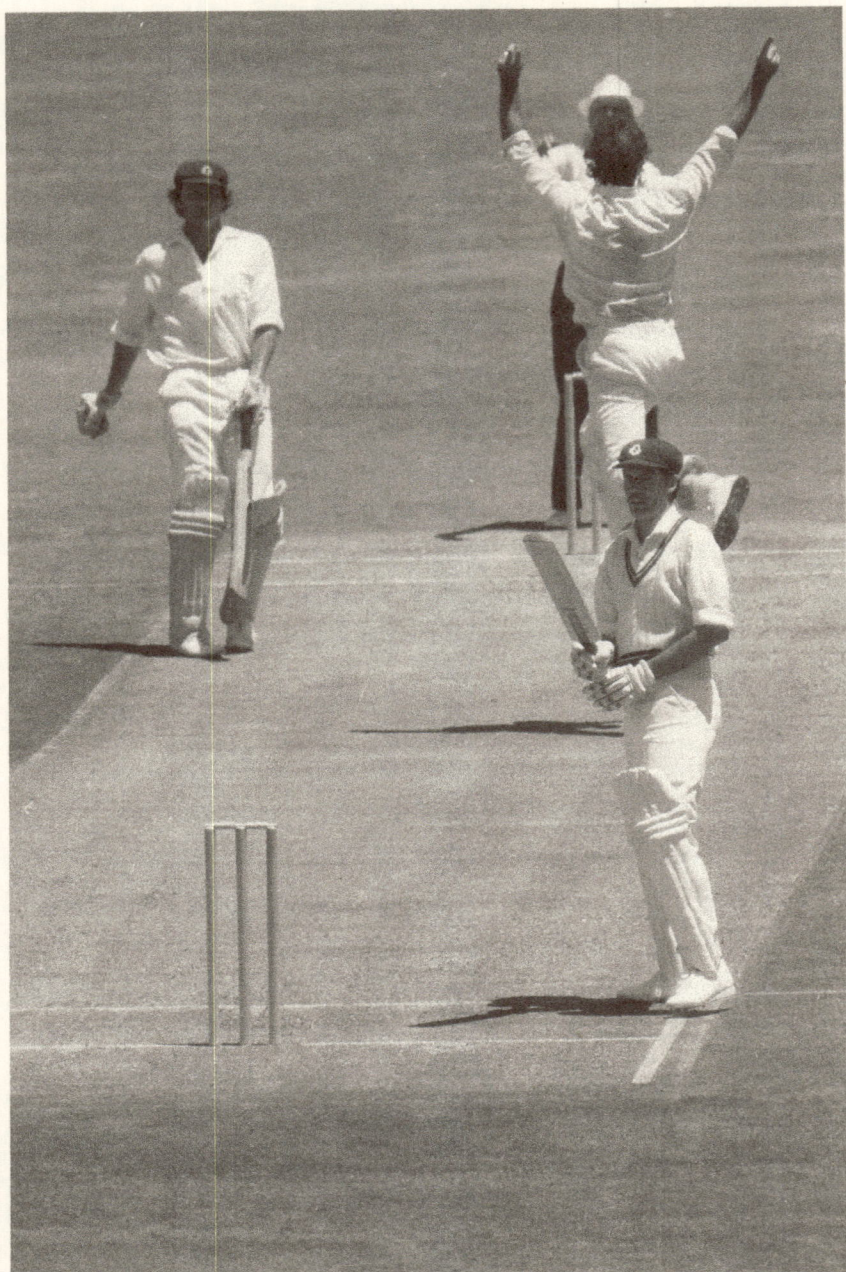

GOTCHA!—Greg Chappell's bemused reaction to the Lillee–Marsh combination that brought about his downfall. Out for just 2.

understandable air of confidence going into the innings. Only 78 needed … yet, so quickly two of the world's best batsmen had been dismissed.

> Viv Richards: After Dennis also got Greg Chappell cheaply, we could see the body language and the energy of the WA players out on the field.

Richie Benaud was across it, too:

> We've got panic stations out there with the batting. Not surprisingly, no one wants to be at Dennis Lillee's end— all a bit keener to have the strike against Mick Malone, I should think.

While Captain Marsh remained clear-headed, refusing to believe in a win until he had seen the last wicket fall, his team-mates around him started to think they could be staring down a historic win.

> Yardley: We were starting to believe we really could do it.

> Serjeant: With two of the world's best bats gone—two guys who potentially were going to win the game off their own bat—that surely sent a message to the Queensland dressing room. We thought we had some semblance of a chance now.

> Hughes: I thought we were now a real chance to post an amazing win.

Spirits may have been soaring out on the field, but there remained a feeling of realism within the home team's ranks. As the dressing room door closed behind Greg Chappell, the cold facts remained—WA still needed 7 wickets and Queensland just 51 runs. It only needed a couple of blokes to stick around and make twenty-odd. Perhaps WA would still go down, but it would be one hell of a fight.

A change of mood

As had been the case with the WA innings, the game was moving very fast. Almost too fast for the man listed to follow Greg Chappell in the Queensland order—experienced campaigner Phil Carlson was literally caught with his pants down:

> As our innings started I was sitting on a chair in the showers at the back of the room, trying to cool off. Next thing I know, Viv's sitting next to me. I said to him, 'What the fuck are you doing here? What's going on?' He said, 'I'm out, man. And David Ogilvie's just out, too.' All of a sudden I'm running around like a mad thing, getting dressed and strapping on my pads. Next thing I'm in. It all happened very quickly.

Queensland vice-captain John Maclean admitted Lillee's work with the ball had thrown a cat among the pigeons with his teammates:

> What Dennis did was superb. We knew he would come out firing, but when he got Viv and Greg in short order something like panic ran through the rest of the group. All of a sudden 78 was more than we thought it was.

Chappell had feared during the break between innings that the pitch would quicken up a little by the afternoon. And he was right. The combined effect of a warm, sunny day and a good drying breeze had not only worked in Lillee's favour, the conditions were also suiting Mick Malone, WA's tall into-the-wind merchant. He had replaced Wayne Clark from the northern end. True to the method of his outstanding career for WA, Malone was swinging the ball both ways prodigiously.

Something of a gentle giant, Malone had also carved out a career as an Australian Rules footballer before turning up to play for WA. And he soon showed his mettle in the summer game. Earning a trip to England in 1977—and, in the one Test match of his career (the Fifth at The Oval) had the rare distinction of claiming 5 wickets (5–63) in his debut innings. He then went to WSC and that was the end of his time in Tests.

Malone would play a vital role in many an innings, and this day at the WACA Ground would be no exception. It was Malone who claimed the next wicket—Carlson trapped leg before for 1 in the eighth over.

Normally a free-scoring player, Carlson had faced 6 deliveries for 1 run. As the WA batsmen had found, it wasn't easy out there. Survival was one thing ... scoring runs was something totally different. And the bulk of that was being done by the cavalier Jones, at that stage on 21 out of 34. Queensland now four down and still 44 runs for victory. The nerves were starting to show in their dressing room.

> Carlson: When I got out and we were 4–34, I thought, hell, things aren't looking good. There was a change of mood among the boys. People started walking around nervously, then somebody told us all to sit still. But that didn't work.

As the nerves continued to jangle in the Queensland camp, Jeff Langley made his way out to the middle. The nephew of well-credentialed Australian wicketkeeper Gil Langley, he had begun his career for South Australia before moving north to improve his opportunities. But though he made two centuries in his twenty-eight first-class games, the diminutive right-hander never quite made it. For the Queensland team to make it in this game, the situation called for something resolute from Langley—a dour rear-guard action in support of the main hope, Jones.

Meanwhile, as Lillee tore into his fifth over (of the eight allowed for any bowler) his captain was staring down a dilemma—whether to keep his danger man going or rest him for a final salvo at the end of the Queensland innings. 'He may well have been stuffed ... they were five pretty dynamic (eight-ball) overs.' It was a decision he decided to share with those nearby.

> Mick Malone: I was standing at second slip and I remember Bacchus turning to all of us in the cordon and asking, 'What do you reckon I should do with FOT?' I said, 'You've got to bowl him out. He's on fire, he's got three, for God's sake bowl him out.' I'm sure I wasn't

alone in this opinion. Bacchus let a ball or two go by and then turned to us and said, 'No boys. I've got to take the big fellow off. If we're going to win this he's got to be bowling at the end.'

There was a second reason why Marsh was reluctant to tell Lillee he was to have a spell. 'I was a little bit hesitant to take him off ... I was more worried about what he would say or do. It was very hard to get the ball off him at the best of times.' In the end the champion took his leave, with figures of 3–12 from five inspirational, match-breaking overs. Up in the commentary box, Ian Chappell, who had enjoyed having Lillee at the head of his Australian attack, was full of praise. 'He's a very competitive bloke with an unbelievably big heart. It's a typical fast-bowling performance from him, and aren't the crowd just loving it.'

No question there were mixed feelings about Marsh's decision to take Lillee out of the attack. Kim Hughes: 'From a captaincy—and psychological—point of view, Bacchus had to make a monumental decision.' Those in the crowd at the southern end, deliriously chanting 'Li-lee ... Li-lee ...' in full voice, were wanting more from their hero. And a plebiscite of the other nine WA players, aside from Marsh and Lillee, would have produced an interesting result—like Mick Malone, I favoured Lillee bowling on, while he was so much on top. Richie Benaud, one of Australia's most astute cricket brains, also demurred. 'I don't think they can afford this. If someone takes a dozen off an over from Wayne Clark then the game's just about gone.'

Far from Marsh's decision to rest Lillee removing an immediate threat for the Queensland batsmen, the lively WA track offered ideal conditions to the men of lesser pace—Malone and Clark (the man chosen to replace Lillee downwind). But what a task for Clark—to fill Lillee's boots from the River End!

Throughout his successful career Clark sent them down at medium-fast pace, based mainly on line and length plus movement off the wicket. He played ten Tests during the World Series Cricket years, claiming 44 wickets at 28.72. That's a healthy strike rate and average. Clark was a quiet, understated man for a pace bowler. Rarely moved to the heat that can be so typical of a fired-up quickie, and just as rarely moved to bounce one through head high. He knew he had a big job to do this day and he approached it this way:

> My aim was to keep the ball up and let it work off the seam. I remember Bacchus saying to me, 'We've got to keep Dennis for the end, we can't just bowl him out. There you are, mate, here's your opportunity.' He had to back his men.

Greg Chappell knew that his team was in a real spot of bother and couldn't help ruing Denis Schuller's two costly overs earlier in the day. But he shared his rival captain's commonsensical approach—it's not over till it's over—and with 6 wickets still in hand Queensland retained some hope. Batsman Alan Jones had watched four teammates now come and go, and he continued his plan to attack at all cost. Apart from the life he was granted, when Yardley and Serjeant combined to spill a catch at backward point, he was enjoying some luck—fortune truly favoured the brave. Ian Chappell assessed Jones's tactics. 'Certainly he's taking every opportunity to play his shots, which is a good thing—although some of them have been rather untoward shots.'

It was the tenth over and he now faced Malone, loping upwind towards him, the score having advanced by one run since Carlson had departed. Malone released, well pitched up, around off stump—and Jones had a lash at it. Richie Benaud: 'There's another one. Langer's the man under it. It's a vital catch … and he's got it! Queensland are in deep trouble, five for 35.'

Langer *was* the man under that lofted shot, but it was far from a sitter.

> Langer: It was swirling quite a bit in the wind. I half fell over backwards in the act of securing it. I remember Bacchus having a bit of a go at me, more or less for trying to make an easy catch look hard. He did concede afterwards that in the circumstances I had every right to tumble backwards.

The fifth Queensland wicket was gone and Alan Jones's hard-earned score of 22 (from 40 balls in a 54-minute stay) wasn't good enough in his captain's eyes once he got back to the dressing room. 'Greg got right up me for the shot I played. It was a bit tense in the rooms, but there still was a feeling within the group that we could win it.'

The batsmen had crossed and four balls later Langley picked up three. At the other end the redoubtable John Maclean settled in for a dog fight. Two singles from Clark's first over downwind, followed by a Malone maiden, settled things down a bit for Queensland. But Clark struck in his next over, the thirteenth. Langley, who had been out there for 24 minutes, was tempted to offer at one that moved away—and was caught by a jubilant Marsh. Benaud: 'A beautiful delivery from Clark! Swinging a lot and finding the outside edge of Langley's bat. Six for 40 and 38 still needed.'

All-rounder Graham Whyte was on his way out to join the dogged John Maclean. Whyte was a tough competitor, handy off-spinner and useful late-order bat. But he was in and out of the Queensland side in a career spanning 1974 to 1985, playing a total of 44 games for 1033 runs and 73 wickets. As he reached the middle you sensed this was about the last roll of the dice for the Maroons. At this point Benaud, too, was sensing something. 'If WA can win this it will be one of the great results in Australian cricket.'

The Godfather

John Maclean

It was like this. Queensland were battling to make a mark in Australian cricket—had been, really, ever since they'd been admitted to the Sheffield Shield competition in 1926—when the board made the bold decision to lure Greg Chappell away from South Australia and asked the incumbent skipper, John Maclean, to concede the captain's role. No, definitely no, he had no problems with standing down. The pair had toured New Zealand with the Australian second side and had become quite close.

Maclean's willingness to step aside clinched the deal for Chappell, who then was able to pinch rising speedster Jeff Thomson away from New South Wales a season later. That coup almost certainly wouldn't have happened if Chappell hadn't already been situated up north. It was all working out for Queensland and for Maclean, who realised that his sacrifice had been worth it. Two outstanding recruits. Understandably,

Maclean was pretty pleased—with himself *and* with the situation. Perhaps the bananabenders weren't going to be a pushover ever again.

Picture, then, a fundraising dinner in Kingaroy (in upstate Queensland) some years later. Greg Ritchie was interviewing Thommo, who, bored with the whole process, said suddenly, 'Get Maclean up here. He got Greg to come and without that I wouldn't have come.' To which Ritchie replied, 'Come on up here, Godfather of Queensland cricket.'

Speaking at Maclean's sixtieth birthday, former Test player Ron Archer, who had actually brokered the deal with Chappell, praised Maclean for so readily standing down as captain. 'It was nothing,' Maclean said, 'we had to get people to change things and winning's much better than losing.' Greg Chappell set Queensland on that course. Gone was the apologetic welcome when WA and other teams arrived in Brisbane. In its place was a frosty front that told you that this mob really meant business.

Sometimes in sport, looks can deceive. Maclean behind the stumps was testament to that. His stout stature is strikingly reminiscent of the physical make-up of Rod Marsh. Both have physiques ideally suited to crouching behind the stumps, rather than prowling the infield ring. He surprised with his agility, making great width to wayward deliveries with ease. With bat in hand he was one of those obstinate buggers you had to almost chisel out. Not totally dour, but nearly. Sound defensive techniques and a massive heart for the battle. Almost above all, he was, in fact still is, a down-to-earth good bloke.

Maclean's build was also well suited to certain positions on the Aussie Rules football field, which is exactly where he played his first competitive sport. Next he went for soccer, ahead of rugby league, then rugby union and baseball. In the summer months, though, it was always cricket. And more cricket. He played two years in the national schoolboys championship, where he came up against Rod Marsh—who would one day stand in his way for a regular spot in the Australian team. Progress continued apace for the young Maclean, selected to make his club first-grade debut at the age of fifteen, and from there he had eyes on the State team. When the great Wally Grout retired, Lew Cooper took over, but in 1968 he broke his thumb and, at the age of twenty-two, Maclean got down behind the stumps for Queensland for the first time.

Maclean had a habit of plastering his face with zinc cream as protection against the sun during those hours out in the middle. And the cream gave him a ghostly look. For this he was given the moniker 'OGO' by his team mates—inspired by 'Oh Ghost Who Walks', from the comic strip 'The Phantom'.

Elevation to the Australian team came in 1978, in the middle of the controversial World Series Cricket stint. Maclean had knocked back a WSC contract in the hope that opportunities would open up for him with Marsh absent from the scene. However, in the first season the selectors overlooked Maclean for NSW gloveman, Steve Rixon, for the five-Test series against India. Maclean finally got the coveted spot in the following summer's Ashes series. He held his place for four Tests, taking eighteen catches, before WA's Kevin Wright was favoured for the role.

Though he was pipped for a more permanent place first by Marsh, and later by Rixon and Wright, his contribution in the Queensland team was constant and always vital. Nothing was more important to him in his time with the Maroons than their first trophy success—victory over WA in the domestic one-day competition in 1975–76. At the WACA Ground the following summer he was hungry for more.

Maclean's tenure with Queensland would last more than a decade, until his retirement in 1979—leaving the game with gas still in the tank. While he may harbour some regrets at having called quits before his time, his contribution to Queensland was outstanding—and enough for him to be accorded the Order of the British Empire (MBE) in 1980.

Battle lines

John Maclean concedes that at 6–40 things were looking really grim. But the WA players knew from experience that they would need a stick of dynamite to get Maclean out and be halfway sure of winning the game. His continued presence at the crease was to be a period of nail-biting for WA. Ric Charlesworth says it all: 'If there was a possible fly in the ointment it was Maclean. He was a handy bat, but experienced and very stubborn.'

The obdurate Maclean was dug in like an oyster on a reef and he found an enterprising ally in off-spinner Graham Whyte— Maclean endorsed the get-on-with-it approach. 'Jonesey had slashed and bashed. And then Whytey, similar to Bruce Yardley [in the WA innings], threw his bat at everything.'

In reality, Queensland were still only one decent partnership away from victory. The odds were about even. Maclean backed himself to defend his wicket, while Whyte backed his eye—and a good dose of luck, playing and missing many times—to move the score along.

Rod Marsh then played what he hoped would be the trump card. He ended Wayne Clark's spell at the River End, as locum for the resting Dennis Lillee. Meantime, Whyte and Maclean had helped themselves to six from Malone's sixth over—and Marsh immediately switched Clark to operate from the northern end. Three off Lillee's first over back and five from his second and Maclean began to see some light at the end of the tunnel. 'So, Whytey and I get it to 61 without further loss. Now we're a chance again!'

By this time tension was mounting to fever pitch. The victory target was almost within reach for Queensland ... and WA still needed four more wickets. The menacing stand had to be broken. Enter the laid-back Clark, now into his seventh over.

DISTURBED—The end of a worrying stand, as Graham Whyte is bowled by Wayne Clark.

He had just one wicket, but it could easily have been more. With his fourth ball he found a way through Whyte's defences to bowl him. Bill Lawry: 'Jagged back and hit the leg stump.' The crowd, overjoyed at 7–61, heaved a healthy sigh of relief. Whyte's contribution—14 runs (only the second Queenslander to reach double figures) from 30 balls—was immeasurable. The partnership an invaluable 21 runs. His departure a real blow to the Maroons' hopes.

Still Maclean was in no mood to give up.

> Even when Whytey went, the target was still close enough. I was feeling I was never going to get out and, perhaps, I could get the side home. We needed only 17 more to win. I still thought we could do it. I played a few streaky shots, but I was leaving them, too. But with FOT, any ball could get you out. I knew that. It was a matter of hanging on grimly and grinding towards the target.

Jeff Thomson was the next batsman in and Maclean's hopes were quickly put to the test. Thommo lasted only 2 balls, also bowled by Clark, playing a wild slog across the line to a straight ball. As Thommo walked off, shaking his head, Bill Lawry waded in. 'A terrible shot, a disgraceful shot from a Test cricketer. He tried to hit him out of the ground, swung too late, clean bowled and it's 8–61. Queensland are gone.' Bob Simpson then cut in, 'Who is it who are gone? Is it WA or Queensland? Only time will tell.' Lawry came again, and he was adamant. 'No, they're gone.' Dissent in the commentary box!

Queensland 8–61. And next man to the crease, wild man Denis Schuller.

The wild one

Denis Schuller

Knowing the heights of Dennis Lillee's competitiveness, I always found it intriguing that he would have developed such a warm relationship—both on and off the field—with the other Denis … Schuller. WA's Dennis was well and truly fully fledged as an international cricketer by the time the 'other' Denis began his first-class career. Sparks flew initially, but soon you could detect a strange connection. Dennis Lillee had a long mane of hair, so did Schuller; Lillee had his shirt buttoned low, revealing a broad expanse of chest, ditto Schuller. Then a relationship developed, but why?

Schuller tells the story.

That all stemmed from the aftermath of a game at the Gabba. We'd won and there was the normal keg in our dressing room afterwards. On these occasions you'd get the odd hangers-on coming in, too. This time, FOT was fiddling with the gun that poured the beer out of the keg. He indicated that the keg was empty. Then this big Dutchman walked up to him and said, 'Where's the beer, mate?' FOT said, 'I don't think we've got any'—and then sprayed him straight in the face with the gun. I could see this bloke was far from pleased and thought it was time for me to apply some of my experience as a bouncer. I got him outside in a hurry and from then on FOT was as you would be with another fast bowler.

Subsequently, I can recall a game in Perth when I was facing FOT and as he's running in he's calling out to me, 'bouncer, bouncer'—and there it goes, about three metres over my head. Then we've got Bacchus calling out to FOT, 'For God's sake, put it close enough for me to catch.'

Schuller was the 'wild one' of my time in first-class cricket. Predictably unpredictable. He could play, though, no doubt about that. In twenty-eight games for the Maroons between 1975 and 1981 he took 66 wickets at the good average of 29.72 with his pacy left-armers. But as a bloke he was just different. He was born in Ipswich, just outside Brisbane, but played a lot in the country after his family shifted out of the capital for business reasons. He started playing senior club cricket in Rockhampton and was chosen for Queensland Country to play games against the West Indies and Pakistan. Schuller picks up the story.

I had a pretty good game against Pakistan and was advised by a coach from school days to try my luck in Adelaide, rather than going to Brisbane. I did well in club cricket there, but I'd had a problem with the law in Queensland and I gathered this didn't go down too well with Sir Donald Bradman. So I packed up and went back to Rockhampton, but I got an encouraging call from Brisbane and moved there to try to break into the Queensland side.

After a couple of good seasons he was picked for Queensland. Schuller's career for Queensland ended at the age of 33 in 1981. He reckons he and Greg Chappell didn't see eye to eye. 'There was too much of the country boy in me for Greg.' Then came the chance to go into the hotel business. He spent six years in Noosa, then time in Mackay and ended up in Rockhampton, where he managed the golf club for ten years—as his wife said, he was the club's best customer after dark. Since then he's been driving a taxi in Rockhampton. Above all, I guess, Denis Schuller's a funny man who is *never* guilty of taking himself—or life—too seriously.

Two wickets left

Two wickets in the space of three balls! Queensland still seventeen runs short of what was rapidly becoming an improbable victory. Denis Schuller was suddenly on his way to the crease. A bowler who would have been forgiven for thinking at the beginning of the innings that with 77 runs to chase he wasn't going to be needed with the bat. And probably *hoping* he wouldn't be—still down in the dumps about his two costly overs earlier in the day. He survived 2 deliveries to end Clark's over ... taking a wild swipe at the first and beaten by a beauty with the second. Bob Simpson summed up the tension that was in danger of smothering the ground. 'Even our scorer here's holding his head in his hands—just wondering what's going on!'

So Maclean was on strike for the beginning of Lillee's eighth over, the last of his allotment for the game. To the WA players the obvious ploy would be for the Queensland vice-captain to retain the strike and see off the champ. Lillee wasn't going to die wondering, though, firing his first ball in short. Maclean swung at it and sent the ball down to Langer at fine leg. The Queensland pair took a single, exposing the lesser-equipped Schuller to face the music. Potentially seven balls from Lillee, who was on fire, desperate to finish his job—and the game.

Lightning was to strike twice on Denis Schuller that day. Now, with the true tailender on strike, the WA players were right on their toes, aware that Maclean would be desperate to get down to the other end to take over against the demon Lillee. Assuming, too, that Schuller would be ready for any opportunity to escape the heat!

> Maclean: I felt sure [Schuller would] understand ...
> he played the ball into the point region and I took off,
> thinking this was the big chance.

Schuller, however, read the situation completely differently, and was none the wiser to Maclean's plan.

> Schuller: There was no pre-conceived urgency about
> getting me off strike. FOT bowled to me, I played
> it comfortably—and the next thing I know OGO's
> standing beside me.

Back to Maclean:

> To my amazement he just stood there. I had to turn and
> go back. Ric Charlesworth threw close to the stumps
> and Kim Hughes bobbled the ball. I lunged at the line
> and, if I didn't get back, I was that close there wasn't
> anything in it. I do believe there was a run in it and

Denis should have gone. I assumed he would have run on my call … but he didn't.

Schuller, who claims not to have heard Maclean's call:

Perhaps I should have gone—better me run out than him! No, I think there was a bit of panic stations.

This account from the fielding team:

Charlesworth: Maclean, desperate to take the strike against Dennis, called for a run. Schuller sent him back and I laid a throw to the stumps at the non-striker's end, where Kim had come in from mid-on and was waiting. To my horror he fumbled the ball, but he recovered to make the run-out.

Hughes: When the ball was in flight I was standing right over the stumps and I was convinced it was going to hit them. So I put my hands in a defensive position, just in case it missed. Almost like a soccer goalie, I was there to stop it and when it hit my hands, instead of the stumps, I had to sort of grab at it. I'm told John Maclean thought he'd made his ground before I got the bails off, but, mate, the umpire wanted to live in Western Australia! Maybe the extra time I took to get the bails off gave him some hope, but I don't know.

It was a moment to bring out the very best in Bill Lawry's career as a television commentator. 'Schuller wouldn't respond to Maclean's call. Tragedy for Queensland. Poor old John Maclean, he survived Dennis Lillee, but he couldn't survive Denis Schuller!'

Maclean took the decision on the chin and walked off, shaking his head in utter bemusement.

HE'S OUT! —Kim Hughes completes the vital run-out of John Maclean.

Maclean: I remain proud of the way I accepted the umpire's decision. Hughes definitely fumbled the ball … But the umpire was up with the appeal and WA were celebrating … Walking off, I was amused in a way, thinking, 'How the hell has this happened?'

Another critical moment in a crazy day's cricket had just played out. Queensland sixteen runs short of the victory target, WA now sweating on the final wicket and with Lillee in the middle of his final over. The run-out was a godsend for the home side, as Jeff Thomson recognised: 'John Maclean was the one to get us there in the end. He could really hang around and milk the runs … virtually playing French cricket.'

Rod Marsh appreciated the 'gift' that had been bestowed on his team:

The run-out of Maclean was pivotal. As long as he was there they remained a chance. He was always a thorn in our side with the bat. He invariably got runs against us.

Maclean had defended stoutly for 44 deliveries—a long stay in the context of this amazing bowlers' game. He'd made only 9 runs, but he'd given his side a real chance.

Queensland 9–62.

The bizarre run-out brought Geoff Dymock out to the non-striker's end. He could only look on while Schuller waited to deal with the situation. With sixteen more runs required for victory and Lillee at the top of his mark, Schuller decided the best way forward would be to go on the offensive. As he waited for Lillee to begin his run-up, Simpson chimed in, 'WA look like they're going to get revenge, but who can tell in this crazy mixed-up game?' Lawry adds: 'Well, Denis Schuller, I wouldn't like my money on him, I'll tell you that. He's just run out his vice-captain.' It was a faint hope for Queensland. Schuller was a *real* tailender. But how would the final act in this drama unfold?

Craig Serjeant, in the gully position, was reading the tea leaves.

> The first ball he faced [from Wayne Clark], Schuller had taken a wild swipe. I was in the gully for an outside edge and was standing accordingly close, to make sure it would carry. I decided that I would be standing far too close for a catch to be easily taken off another such slash, especially at Dennis's extra pace. I looked over to Bacchus and nodded to him that I wanted to take a big step back. He nodded back and I moved at least a metre back.

In the heat of the moment, Marsh wasn't going to stamp any authority. He trusted his man: 'Gully's a position where you get a feel for things. I didn't argue with him.'

For his part, Schuller had sized up his options.

> The field was pretty well packed on the off-side and FOT knew where to bowl, obviously. It wasn't a case of me working it around to mid-wicket. I should have gone flat chat at it, though—probably a thick edge would have been a bit better than hitting the bloody thing in the middle and straight down gully's throat.

> Serjeant: When it did come, I saw it with enough time to get my hands in a position in front of my face and the ball lodged firmly. Standing in the original position, I reckon I mightn't have caught it.

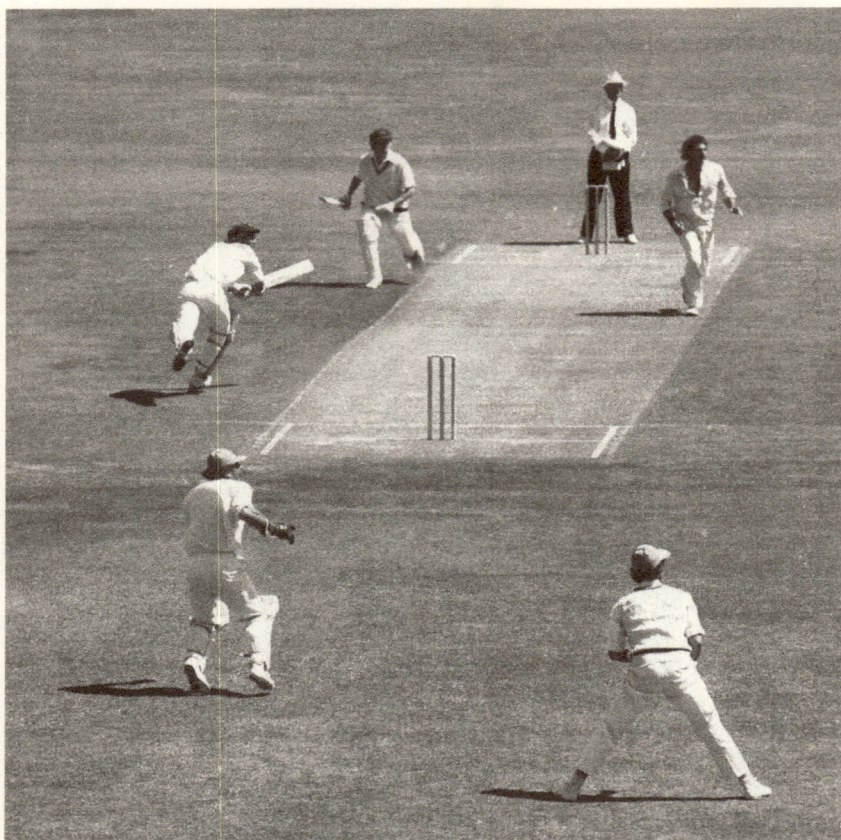

GAME OVER—Denis Schuller heads off for a run, but it's to no
avail—he's out, caught off Dennis Lillee, and WA are the winners
of this extraordinary game.

Bill Lawry's customary ebullience on the microphone was at
its best. 'WA has bowled Queensland out for 62. An unbelievable performance! And what a cricketer Dennis Lillee is ... as
children pour onto the ground.'

Queensland's final four wickets had fallen for 1 run in
8 balls. The unwinnable game had been won (by the 'comfortable' margin of 15 runs) and the unlosable game had been lost!

In the final analysis, it was the great heart and will of Dennis
Lillee that won the day. He had refused to accept that WA

couldn't successfully defend 77 runs and went out to prove his point. Which he did, admirably. He took 4 wickets—including those of two of the world's finest batsmen—off 7 eight-ball overs and 3 balls. He was Bob Simpson's Man-of-the-Match. 'He set the sparkle, set the fire and he brought it in.' Tongue in cheek, the 'other' Denis (Schuller) disagrees. 'I should have been Man-of-the-Match—for WA. Gave away 22 runs off 2 overs, ran out John Maclean, the man who could have won the game for us, and made a duck!'

Of course, Lillee *was* named Man-of-the-Match after that performance, but he wasn't about to take all the credit:

> Let's not forget the job that Wayne Clark did with the ball, initially from the other end, but then after I took a spell from the southern end. He bowled immaculate stuff that swung away and cut back. Plus, the fielding was so good. A wonderful catch by Mick Malone and a beautiful pick-up-and-throw by Ric Charlesworth to run Maclean out when he was possibly going to lead a late charge to victory.

Amen!

Can you believe it?

Craig Serjeant triumphantly threw the ball into the air. It was all over! The WA players raced to mob the hero of the day, Dennis Lillee, while Denis Schuller and Geoff Dymock quietly departed the scene of destruction.

And pandemonium broke loose around the WACA Ground. Large numbers of the crowd invaded the field. It was a moment when belief hung suspended. In a trice we were all surrounded. Plenty of pats on the back.

Schuller and Dymock opened their dressing room door to an air of pervading numbness and devastation. But the pragmatist in their captain, Greg Chappell, recognised something within the ignominy of such a defeat.

Inexperienced sides can find ways to lose, whereas it's the opposite with the more seasoned team. We bowled well, but when it came to making a meagre amount of runs we perhaps succumbed to the pressures. It was devastating for us, but the loss was a reflection of the fragility of our group at the time. I knew better things were to come, and they did.

His opposing number, Rod Marsh:

> I was just thinking about the bowling changes and who should be fielding where … until the last wicket fell. When it was over and I had finally battled my way through the crowd to reach the dressing room—and was able to gather my thoughts—I remember thinking, 'Actually, we won that quite easily!' That was the first thing that came to my mind.

It was a conclusion typical of the man's down-to-earth nature—and his sharp sense of humour! At least a thousand ecstatic fans milled around outside the dressing room. Out in the middle, ground staff watered in the pitch that had borne so many demons, yet played such a role in creating a game that would become immortal.

In both dressing rooms, the teams were in a state of complete disbelief.

> Maclean: When I got back to our dressing room after being dismissed—nine down and still sixteen runs short of victory—the atmosphere was shell-shocked … with Viv and Greg in the side most of us thought we'd walk to the target and go on to the final. We'll play a cameo role here. This is all over. Then Denis Schuller goes the next ball and it's finished. So, instead of celebrating we're sitting around wondering what the hell has happened?

MOBBED—Members of the crowd, young and old, surround two of
their heroes ... Dennis Lillee and Bruce Yardley.

Hughes: I remember sheer mayhem in our rooms as the win, and its importance, began to sink in on us. We had come from a truly hopeless position to win and, as it turned out, to win comfortably.

Serjeant: It was surreal, a euphoric moment in our sporting lives.

WA selector, Lawrie Sawle: In the bar afterwards I ran into a mate, who was quietly sipping on a beer. He said to me, 'I don't know what all the excitement's about … the game wasn't even close!'

Viv Richards: It will live in my mind forever what happened that day. I am sure that the conditions and the state of the game played on our minds. However, all credit must go to the team fielding second in those circumstances—for believing in themselves and for being able to deliver with the ball. Whenever I come to Australia, inevitably folks from WA want to remind me of that game. Not only those who saw it, but also those who played in it!

Jeff Thomson: It was one of those games where a slight lapse could put you into a position where it was impossible to get out. A poor over, a dropped catch. We lost, but we've never really worried about it. We'd beaten WA by a small margin in the final the year before. It simply wasn't our turn.

When the dust settled on the game, the figures truly were incredible. In two completed innings only five batsmen—Ric Charlesworth, Rob Langer, Bruce Yardley, Alan Jones and Graham Whyte—reached double figures. And ten batsmen failed to score. And in a game scheduled to last 80 eight-ball overs, only 43 were used. Queensland used five bowlers, WA only three. And, not surprisingly, neither captain had the need to call on a spinner—though each side had included one: Whyte for Queensland; Yardley for WA.

THE HERO—Dennis Lillee, after being named Man-of-the-Match.

Consider this, too. Dennis Lillee carried two injury problems into the game—recurring back trouble and a groin strain. As he did so many times in his illustrious career, he turned a blind eye to these concerns:

> I knew deep in my heart my back could go at any minute. I guess I increased the chances of that happening. I set out to bowl as fast and as well as I could. Everything fell into place and we did the impossible. It was a fairy tale—like a dream come true.

Here's what the final scorecard looked like:

Western Australia

		R	M	B
Laird	c Ogilvie b Thomson	8	15	11
Charlesworth	lbw b Carlson	25	66	55
Langer	b Dymock	15	44	31
Hughes	b Carlson	0	18	6
Serjeant	lbw b Dymock	0	6	6
Marsh	c Richards b Dymock	0	1	1
Brayshaw	run out	5	37	28
Yardley	c Maclean b Chappell	19	21	23
Lillee	c Jones b Chappell	0	1	3
Malone	not out	0	11	3
Clark	c Thomson b Carlson	0	2	5
Extras		5		
Total		77		

Fall of wickets: 1–8 (Laird), 2–50 (Langer), 3–50 (Charlesworth), 4–51 (Serjeant), 5–51 (Marsh), 6–51 (Hughes), 7–76 (Yardley), 8–76 (Lillee), 9–77 (Brayshaw), 10–77 (Clark).

Bowling

	O	M	R	W
Thomson	4	1	10	1
Dymock	8	2	20	3
Schuller	2	0	30	3
Carlson	5.5	1	17	0
Chappell	3	1	3	2

Queensland innings

		R	M	B
Richards	b Lillee	0	4	6
Jones	c Langer b Malone	22	54	40
Ogilvie	c Malone b Lillee	9	19	13
Chappell	c Marsh b Lillee	2	8	7
Carlson	lbw Malone	1	8	6
Langley	c Marsh b Clark	4	24	12
Maclean	run out	9	59	44
Whyte	b Clark	14	35	30
Thomson	b Clark	0	1	2
Schuller	c Serjeant b Lillee	0	5	4
Dymock	not out	0	1	0
Extras		1		
Total		**62**		

Fall of wickets: 1–0 (Richards), 2–23 (Ogilvie), 3–27 (Chappell), 4–34 (Carlson), 5–35 (Jones), 6–40 (Langley), 7–61 (Whyte), 8–61 (Thomson), 9–62 (Maclean), 10–62 (Schuller).

Bowling

	O	M	R	W
Lillee	7.3	1	21	4
Clark	7	1	21	2
Malone	6	1	19	2

Attendance: 9463

Aftermath

One of the joys—call it a fringe benefit, if you like—of playing interstate cricket in those days was the (generally) free fraternisation with the opposition after the hours of play. There were rules. The side batting for most of the day would visit the fielding team's rooms—you'd let 15 minutes go by before knocking on the door, and you'd have emptied your fridge of drinks (beer and soft) and brought the contents with you. From that moment on, the hostilities of the day's play were put to one side. You were there to meet new faces, to greet old faces and to have a good old chat about the game, and games that had been and were to come. If you asked the right questions of the right person, quite often you could pick up some information about a player you were due to meet. A matter of trading thoughts.

It was social, it was fun and it was an important part of the fabric of the game at that time. And all but the Victorians encouraged it and participated in it wholeheartedly. We always thought the Vics didn't come into our room—or welcome us into their domain—because their captain, Bill Lawry, was such a tartar and tough competitor that such an exchange of pleasantries would have been seen as a sign of weakness in the face of the opposition. Having said that, we'd always get a knock on the door from one of his men. Paul Sheahan, bottle of beer in hand, would step over the threshold, wait for the ribaldry (about his teammates) to die down and then walk in and do what the rest of them should have taken a pleasure in doing.

> Kim Hughes: That was the beauty of those days. You were pretty well always able to rub shoulders with the opposition. It was a time when young cricketers could learn a lot from the more senior players, both in their own side and from the opposition.

Queensland had a quaint custom at the end of a game at the Gabba. They'd open the doors—*and* a keg of beer—and let it all hang out for an hour or so. Because Ian Chappell was a devotee of the practice, sometimes the South Australians would want to stay longer than made sense, especially if you had to front up again the next day. The NSW room at the SCG was slightly different. Comfy cane chairs were set out in two semicircles facing the window looking out on the ground. When I was a youngster in the side, the inner circle would be the domain of the likes of Brian Booth and Norm O'Neill, plus senior WA players like Barry Shepherd and Graham McKenzie. The outer circle would house slightly lesser luminaries, while the new chums stood at the rear—and hung on every word that emanated from the inner sanctums.

Given all of this, it was a natural thing that when all the emotions of The Miracle Match had finally settled down, the Queensland players opened their door to the victors. It was as though both winners and losers realised that they had all taken part in something special—a once-in-a-lifetime game.

> Viv Richards: You played hard on the field, but you could share a cold beer afterwards with the opposition. It tended to replace the energy you had expended out there on the field. We had all participated in an amazing game and it was a tribute to Greg Chappell—and a reminder of his ideals of sportsmanship—that he would welcome the WA players into our dressing room that afternoon.

> Craig Serjeant: It seemed there were no long faces in the room that afternoon. What had begun as an embarrassment for us turned out to be a spectacle that nobody who was at the ground that day would ever forget.

It's funny how things can stick in your mind! Of all the memories that endure of that incredible one day in my life, one of the strongest relates to a visitor to the Queensland room during the post-game gathering. His name was Donald Rudolph Weekes, and he was an old friend of Viv Richards's from Barbados. And no more than 15 minutes after the game ended, he burst in as though he owned the place, making a bee-line for Richards. Viv started giggling. 'Donny Weekes, Donny Weekes, he's everywhere!' The story had gone around that Viv had done some boxing in New York—and Donny claimed he was his trainer. He also reckoned he taught Muhammad Ali to 'rope-a-dope' and all that sort of stuff. Next thing he's throwing straight lefts at Viv and saying, 'You blinked.' So the mood in the room lightened a bit, with this sudden appearance. The Queenslanders almost found the ability to laugh!

The thing about Donny Weekes, he had this wonderful ability to make the most of a story. I had met Donny a short time before—and had been sucked in by his tales … which included, in addition to his Muhammad Ali connection, making 781 not out in an innings in India, swimming the English Channel in record time, coaching the United States fencing team, going to Hollywood as an actor and screenwriter, acting in *Othello* and having a personal art exhibition in Paris. Most, if not all, of his outlandish claims have been proven to be no more than bunkum. But they were good enough for mugs like me to fill his cuttings file … and soon gain some quirky sort of credibility.

When it was time to return to our room and pack our gear, we all began to reflect on a truly amazing day—one none of us would ever forget.

Ric Charlesworth has tasted more success in sport than most. He has some interesting perspectives on that magical day at the WACA Ground:

> How does that game rate with all the high-level sporting experiences I have had? Well it was always exciting to be part of a team that won the Sheffield Shield, but there was so much more intensity in this game. You just had to win it, there was no second chance. It was more like a football match than a cricket game. It was such a topsy-turvy day. We were so disappointed, then so elated. In the field that day we had so few runs to play with that every bad ball, every mistake, was magnified.

Kim Hughes brought another slant to the discussion—one that was never far from anyone's minds during those years leading up to WSC:

> Talking about the money we got that day—and it was the same for all of us, from the captain down—we later found out that the bloke on the gate, a lovely old fellow, got more than we each did for playing! And it was a huge game, televised Australia-wide and featuring such world stars as Richards, Chappell, Thomson, Lillee and Marsh, with a big crowd in attendance. Unbelievable entertainment, and all we got for the part we played was eighteen bucks. A ten, a five, a two and a one—all notes in those days!

And the competition sponsor actually paid more money to each of a handful of 'dolly birds' who floated around the ground during the game, promoting its name and products. It was a good thing that money wasn't king for cricketers back in 1976.

When the WA innings ended so disastrously, there had been talk of a late-afternoon gathering at the home of one of the players. This talk went on the backburner after Dennis Lillee fired up his teammates to consider the unlikely victory, which came at 2.28 pm. However, when the excitement started to settle and the drinks ran out in the Queensland room, there was indeed a barbecue for the team and their wives.

Let Kim Hughes pick up the story:

> I was only twenty-two at the time and my ability to hold alcohol wasn't all that great. However, we all got caught up in the euphoria of the game and had quite a few beers. By the time the grog ran out, for me it was

then a matter of getting to a follow-up function at Ian Brayshaw's place in Trigg. I probably shouldn't have been behind the wheel of my blue Hillman Super Minx. But there I was, tonking along Karrinyup Road, no more than a kilometre from my destination, when a couple of policemen pulled me over. I was still in my creams and studs, barely able to tell them my name. They asked where I was going and I told them that I was heading to a celebration party at Sticks's place, just around the corner. They said, 'Well, give us your keys. You'd better get in here and we'll deliver you.' So I got the Hillman off the road, gave them the keys, hopped in the back of the paddy wagon and they took me there. Then they knocked on the door and said, 'We've got a bloke here who's a bit lost. Look after him.' And pushed me in. That was that.

Finis piece

The unlikely victory over Queensland hoisted WA into the final against Victoria 42 days later, played at the MCG before 32,908 fans—a record attendance at a domestic one-day game in Australia. A bit like the semifinal, one side (Victoria) had the game all wrapped up. That is, until something akin to divine intervention came to WA's rescue for a second time that season. Rod Marsh had won the toss and sent the Vics in to bat. The home side gave a steady team performance in setting WA to make 165 for victory.

Bowling like the wind from the Southern Stand end, Alan Hurst ripped into WA's top order. He'd taken the wicket of Kim Hughes, to have WA 3–38, when I went out to face some of his chin music. The Vics were on a roll and noise from the parochial crowd was so loud that you couldn't make yourself heard in asking the umpire for guard. As for calling for running between the wickets—hand signals only. Bruce Laird had made 20 at the top of the innings, but Ric Charlesworth, Rob Langer and then Hughes had gone in short order. I added 21, but WA's batting was on a slippery slide and when Bruce Yardley went for a duck the situation was nigh-on impossible at 7–74.

Then the tide turned. Mick Malone, a handy tailender at best, joined Craig Serjeant. The pair added 51, before Serjeant went for an invaluable 38. WA now 8–125 … and a slight chance of a sneaking victory. Dennis Lillee and Malone had advanced the score by 14 when Lillee was run out, to the dismay of the rest of us in the dressing room. The task for the last pair of Malone and Wayne Clark (a real bunny!): to score 26 runs and not to run out of overs thinking about it.

Lillee remembers the scene in the WA dressing room as the run chase unfolded:

> We had a thing going, 'we can't win this one, we can't possibly get these runs, but don't move from your seat'—reflecting a dressing room superstition that if you moved from your seat in a tense situation you might bring about the loss of a wicket.

So we all stayed put, crossed our legs and our fingers and watched in fascination as the two unlikely heroes went about winning the game. Malone, a resolute competitor if ever there was one, shouldered the responsibility of scoring the runs, while Clark made sure he hung on at the other end. With the third ball of the final eight-ball over, Malone took an inside edge off medium-pacer Trevor Laughlin. The ball shaved the leg stump and rolled into the gutter by the sightscreen, just out of the reach of a diving, sprawling Ray Bright. Almost unbelievably, Malone had contributed 47.

WA had won!

Literally seconds after the end of the game, the then secretary of the Victorian Cricket Association made an amazing entry to the sanctuary of the WA dressing room. Aghast at yet another Houdini act by this indomitable team, he burst through the door and shouted, 'That's it. I'm revoking your passports. You're all staying here!' David Richards, who would go on to be chief executive officer of the Australian Cricket Board, then to the lofty position of CEO of the International Cricket Council, was utterly exasperated. These cowboys from the West had done it again. Pulled victory from the jaws of certain defeat. On top of the team's incredible performance in winning The Miracle Match, it was too much for him!

When captain Marsh held the Gillette Cup aloft after the presentations, he must have known that all his Christmases had come at once. Really, there had been *two* miracle results for WA that campaign … but there was only one Miracle Match!

Acknowledgements

Quite some story, eh? However, it wouldn't have happened without the willing acquiescence of a long line of interviewees. Their names are listed in the 'Author's note' earlier. To them all, I express my gratitude. And I particularly want to thank the Queenslanders—who were on the losing side, but were big enough to talk openly to me about that incredible game.

My sincere thanks, too, to Peter Henley. A chance meeting in Melbourne resulted in an introduction to Sandy Grant of Hardie Grant Publishing. Sandy encouraged me to proceed with the project and the rest, as they say, is history. Thanks to Emma Hutchinson for her invaluable contribution as editor.

Finally, thanks to my son Mark who challenged me to write this book.

For research purposes, I referred to the following books:

Sir Vivian Richards and Bob Harris, *Sir Vivian: The Definitive Biography*. London, Michael Joseph, 2000.

Ashley Mallett, *Thommo Speaks Out: The Authorised Biography of Jeff Thomson*. Crows Nest, NSW, Allen & Unwin, 2009.

Christian Ryan, *Golden Boy: Kim Hughes and the Bad Old Days of Australian Cricket*. Crows Nest, NSW, Allen & Unwin, 2009.

Bruce Yardley, *Roo's Book*. Wyalkatchem, WA, 2011.

About the author

Ian Brayshaw is a journalist-cum-author, who has written or co-written some 25 books on sports and sports heroes. He played cricket for WA for 17 years, and in 1967 became only the third bowler in Sheffield Shield history to take all ten wickets in an innings. The feat has never been repeated since in Shield cricket.

At the time of his retirement in 1978, Brayshaw was viewed by some to be the best player to not have played cricket for Australia. Brayshaw was awarded an MBE in 1978 for his services to sport.